Scoring High

Stanford Achievement Test

A Test Prep Program

Book 2

Columbus, OH

The McGraw·Hill Companies

www.sra4kids.com

 SRA

Send all inquiries to:
SRA/McGraw-Hill
4400 Easton Commons
Columbus, OH 43219

ISBN 0-07-584103-7

11 12 13 14 15 16 17 18 19 RHR 15 14 13 12 11

The **McGraw·Hill** Companies

Book 2

On Your Way to
Scoring High Stanford Achievement Test

Family Letter

Greetings!

Your child, like many students across the country, will take standardized tests throughout his or her educational experience. Standardized tests are administered for several reasons.

- It gives us a snapshot of what your child has learned (achieved). It is one of many ways we assess the skills and knowledge of students because no one test or assessment tool can give an accurate, ongoing picture of your child's development.

- We use the Stanford Achievement Test to help us determine where to strengthen our curriculum to better meet the needs of the students. It also helps us see if we are meeting the learning goals we set previously.

In order to give students the best opportunity to prepare for standardized achievement tests, we will be using SRA/McGraw-Hill's test preparation program, *Scoring High* on the *Stanford Achievement Test.* Why will we be spending time using this program?

- Test-taking skills can be learned. When preparing, we focus on such skills as reading and listening carefully to directions; budgeting time; answering the easy questions first so you can spend more time on the harder ones; eliminating answer choices that are obviously wrong, and more. These are life skills that students will take with them and use again and again.

- Preparing for standardized tests assures that students won't be surprised by the format of the test. They won't be worried about the type of questions they will see, or how hard the questions will be. They'll know how to fill in answers appropriately. These, and other skills learned ahead of time, will free students to focus on the content of the test and thus give a much more accurate picture of what they know.

How can you help?

- Talk to us here at school if you have any questions. Remember, we are a team with the **same** goals in mind—the improvement of your child's educational experience.

- Encourage reading at home, and spend time together talking about what you read.

Please feel free to contact me if you have any questions.

Sincerely,

_____

Your child's teacher

Scoring High on the Stanford Achievement Test
A program that teaches achievement test behaviors

Scoring High Stanford Achievement Test is designed to prepare students for these tests. The program provides instruction and practice in word study, reading, mathematics, spelling, language, and listening skills. *Scoring High* also familiarizes students with the kinds of test formats and directions that appear on the tests and teaches test-taking strategies that promote success.

Students who are used to a comfortable learning environment are often unaccustomed to the structured setting in which achievement tests are given. Even students who are used to working independently may have difficulty maintaining a silent, sustained effort or following directions that are read to a large group. *Scoring High*, with its emphasis on group instruction, teaches these test-taking skills systematically.

Using *Scoring High* to help prepare students for the Stanford Achievement Test will increase the probability of your students doing their best on the tests. Students' self-confidence will be at a maximum, and their proficiency in the skills tested will be higher as a result of the newly learned test-taking strategies and increased familiarity with test formats.

Scoring High can be used effectively along with your regular reading, language arts, and mathematics curriculums. By applying subject-area skills in the context of the test-taking situation, students will not only strengthen their skills, but they also will accumulate a reserve of test-taking strategies.

Eight Student Books for Grades 1–8

To choose the most appropriate book for each student, match the level of the Stanford Achievement Test that the student will take to the corresponding *Scoring High* book.

Grade Levels	Test Levels
Book 1	Primary 1
Book 2	Primary 2
Book 3	Primary 3
Book 4	Intermediate 1
Book 5	Intermediate 2
Book 6	Intermediate 3
Book 7	Advanced 1
Book 8	Advanced 2

Sequential Skill Development

Each student book is organized into units reflecting the subject areas covered in the corresponding levels of the Stanford Achievement Test. This book covers word study, reading, mathematics, spelling, language, and listening skills. Each lesson within a unit focuses on several subject-area skills and the test-taking strategies that complement the skills. The last lesson in each unit is designed to give students experience in taking an achievement test in that subject area.

The Test Practice section at the end of each book also provides practice in taking achievement tests and will increase students' confidence in their test-taking skills.

Note: The lessons in this book are arranged in the order in which comparable items appear on the Stanford Achievement Test. You may find it helpful to review the lessons and administer them in the order that is most appropriate for the reading level of your students.

Features of the Student Lessons

Each student lesson in subject-area skills contains:

- A Sample(s) section including directions and one or more teacher-directed sample questions
- A Tip(s) section providing test-taking strategies
- A practice section

Each Test Yourself lesson at the end of a unit is designed like an achievement test in the unit's subject areas.

How the Teacher's Edition Works

Because a program that teaches test-taking skills as well as subject-area skills may be new to your students, the Teacher's Edition makes a special effort to provide detailed lesson plans. Each lesson lists subject-area and test-taking skills. In addition, teaching suggestions are provided for handling each part of the lesson—Sample(s), Tip(s), and the practice items. The text for the subject-area and Test Yourself lessons is designed to help students become familiar with following oral directions and with the terminology used on the tests.

Before you begin Lesson 1, you should use the Orientation Lesson on pages xv–xviii to acquaint students with the program organization and the procedure for using the student book.

Test-taking Skills

Analyzing answer choices

Analyzing a problem

Avoiding overanalysis of answer choices

Choosing a picture to answer a question

Comparing answer choices

Computing carefully

Considering every answer choice

Converting items to a workable format

Finding the answer without computing

Following complex directions

Following oral directions

Following printed directions

Identifying and using key words, figures, and numbers to find the answer

Indicating that the correct answer is not given

Indicating that an item has no mistakes

Listening carefully

Marking the right answer as soon as it is found

Performing the correct operation

Reasoning from facts and evidence

Referring to a graphic

Referring to a passage to answer questions

Rereading questions

Searching for multiple errors

Skimming a passage

Skipping difficult items and returning to them later

Staying with the first answer

Subvocalizing answer choices

Taking the best guess when unsure of the answer

Transferring numbers accurately

Understanding unusual item formats

Using charts and graphs

Using context to find the answer

Working methodically

Reading Skills

Choosing the best title for a story

Deriving word or phrase meaning

Drawing conclusions

Identifying compound words

Identifying informational resources

Identifying synonyms

Identifying word meaning from sentence context

Identifying words with more than one meaning

Making inferences

Making predictions

Matching phonemes

Recognizing the author's purpose

Recognizing contractions

Recognizing details

Recognizing feelings

Recognizing setting

Recognizing suffixes

Understanding the lesson of a story

Understanding the main idea

Understanding reasons

Understanding sequence

Mathematics Skills

Adding whole numbers

Comparing and ordering numbers

Completing number or shape patterns

Counting

Identifying the best measurement unit

Interpreting tables and graphs

Naming numerals

Recognizing arithmetic fact families

Recognizing basic shapes

Recognizing equivalent operations

Recognizing fractional parts

Recognizing numbers

Recognizing ordinal numbers

Recognizing the value of coins

Solving number puzzles

Solving oral word problems

Subtracting whole numbers

Telling time

Understanding the base-ten system

Understanding a calendar

Understanding mathematics language

Understanding measurement

Understanding number sentences

Understanding place value

Understanding plane figures

Understanding probability

Understanding symmetry

Using a number line

Language and Listening Skills

Answering questions about an orally presented
story

Choosing correctly used words

Choosing a picture to answer questions about an
orally presented story

Identifying the best sentence to add to a paragraph

Identifying correct capitalization

Identifying correct composition strategies

Identifying correct punctuation

Identifying correctly formed sentences

Identifying incorrectly spelled words

Identifying the main reason for a paragraph

Identifying a sentence that does not fit in a
paragraph

Identifying synonyms for orally presented words in
context

Scope and Sequence: Test-taking Skills

	UNIT 1	2	3	4	5	6	7	8	9
Analyzing answer choices	✓								✓
Analyzing a problem					✓				✓
Avoiding overanalysis of answer choices						✓			✓
Choosing a picture to answer a question								✓	✓
Comparing answer choices		✓				✓	✓		✓
Computing carefully					✓				✓
Considering every answer choice		✓				✓			✓
Converting items to a workable format					✓				✓
Finding the answer without computing				✓					✓
Following complex directions	✓								✓
Following oral directions	✓							✓	✓
Following printed directions		✓							✓
Identifying and using key words, figures, and numbers to find the answer			✓	✓					✓
Indicating that the correct answer is not given					✓				✓
Indicating that an item has no mistakes							✓		✓
Listening carefully				✓			✓	✓	✓
Marking the right answer as soon as it is found				✓			✓	✓	✓
Performing the correct operation					✓				✓
Reasoning from facts and evidence			✓						✓
Referring to a graphic				✓					✓
Referring to a passage to answer questions			✓				✓		✓
Rereading questions			✓						✓
Searching for multiple errors						✓			✓
Skimming a passage			✓						✓
Skipping difficult items and returning to them later		✓							✓
Staying with the first answer					✓		✓	✓	✓
Subvocalizing answer choices	✓					✓	✓		✓
Taking the best guess when unsure of the answer	✓	✓		✓				✓	✓
Transferring numbers accurately					✓				✓
Understanding unusual item formats	✓							✓	✓
Using charts and graphs				✓					✓
Using context to find the answer		✓					✓		✓
Working methodically	✓	✓	✓	✓	✓	✓	✓		✓

Scope and Sequence: Reading Skills

	UNIT								
	1	2	3	4	5	6	7	8	9
Choosing the best title for a story			✓						
Deriving word or phrase meaning			✓						
Drawing conclusions			✓						✓
Identifying compound words	✓								✓
Identifying informational resources			✓						
Identifying synonyms		✓							✓
Identifying word meaning from sentence context		✓							✓
Identifying words with more than one meaning		✓							✓
Making inferences			✓						✓
Making predictions			✓						✓
Matching phonemes	✓								✓
Recognizing the author's purpose			✓						
Recognizing contractions	✓								
Recognizing details			✓						
Recognizing feelings									✓
Recognizing setting									✓
Recognizing suffixes	✓								✓
Understanding the lesson of a story									✓
Understanding the main idea			✓						✓
Understanding reasons			✓						✓
Understanding sequence			✓						✓

Scope and Sequence: Mathematics Skills

	UNIT								
	1	2	3	4	5	6	7	8	9
Adding whole numbers					✓				✓
Comparing and ordering numbers				✓					
Completing number or shape patterns									✓
Counting				✓					✓
Identifying the best measurement unit									✓
Interpreting tables and graphs				✓					✓
Naming numerals									✓
Recognizing arithmetic fact families				✓					
Recognizing basic shapes				✓					
Recognizing equivalent operations									✓
Recognizing fractional parts				✓					✓
Recognizing numbers				✓					
Recognizing ordinal numbers				✓					✓
Recognizing the value of coins				✓					
Solving number puzzles				✓					
Solving oral word problems				✓	✓				✓
Subtracting whole numbers					✓				✓
Telling time				✓					✓
Understanding the base-ten system				✓					
Understanding a calendar				✓					
Understanding mathematics language				✓					
Understanding measurement									✓
Understanding number sentences				✓					✓
Understanding place value				✓					✓
Understanding plane figures									✓
Understanding probability				✓					✓
Understanding symmetry				✓					✓
Using a number line									✓

Scope and Sequence: Language and Listening Skills

	UNIT								
	1	2	3	4	5	6	7	8	9
Answering questions about an orally presented story								✓	✓
Choosing correctly used words							✓		✓
Choosing a picture to answer questions about an orally presented story								✓	✓
Identifying the best sentence to add to a paragraph							✓		✓
Identifying correct capitalization							✓		✓
Identifying correct composition strategies							✓		✓
Identifying correct punctuation							✓		✓
Identifying correctly formed sentences							✓		✓
Identifying incorrectly spelled words						✓			✓
Identifying the main reason for a paragraph							✓		✓
Identifying a sentence that does not fit in a paragraph							✓		✓
Identifying synonyms for orally presented words in context								✓	✓

Orientation Lesson

Focus
Understanding the purpose and structure of *Scoring High Stanford Achievement Test*

Note: Before you begin Lesson 1, use this introductory lesson to acquaint the students with the program orientation and procedures for using this book.

Say Taking a test is something you do many times during each school year. What kind of tests have you taken? *(math tests, reading tests, spelling tests, daily quizzes, etc.)* Have you ever taken an achievement test that covers many subjects? An achievement test shows how well you are doing in these subjects compared to other students in your grade. Do you know how achievement tests are different from the regular tests you take in class? *(Many students take them on the same day; special pencils, books, and answer sheets are used; etc.)* Some students get nervous when they take achievement tests. Has this ever happened to you?

Encourage the students to discuss their feelings about test taking. Point out that almost everyone feels anxious or worried when facing a test-taking situation.

Display the cover of *Scoring High Stanford Achievement Test*.

Say Here is a new book you'll be using for the next several weeks. The book is called *Scoring High Stanford Achievement Test*.

Distribute the books to the students.

Say This book will help you improve your word study, reading, mathematics, spelling, language, and listening skills. It will also help you gain

Scoring High
Stanford Achievement Test
A Test Prep Program

Book 2

SRA

the confidence and test-taking skills you need to do well on achievement tests. What does the title say you will be doing when you finish this book? *(scoring high)* Scoring high on achievement tests is what this program is all about. If you learn the skills taught in this book, you will be ready to do your best on the Stanford Achievement Test.

Inform the students about the testing date if you know when they will be taking the Stanford Achievement Test. Then make sure the students understand that the goal of their *Scoring High* books is to improve their word study, reading, mathematics, spelling, language, listening, and other skills.

Tell the students to turn to the table of contents at the front of their books.

Say This page is a progress chart. It shows the contents of the book. How many units are there? *(9)* Let's read the names of the units together. *(Read the names of the units aloud.)* In these units, you will learn word study, reading, mathematics, spelling, language, listening, and test-taking skills. The last lesson in each unit is called Test Yourself. It reviews what you have learned in the unit. In Unit 9, the Test Practice section, you will have a chance to use all the skills you have learned on tests that are similar to real achievement tests. This page will also help you keep track of the lessons you have completed. Do you see the box beside each lesson number? When you finish a lesson, you will write your score in the box to show your progress.

Make sure the students understand the information presented on this page.

Say Now let's look at two of the lessons. Turn to Lesson 1a on page 1.

Check to be sure the students have found page 1.

Say The lesson number and title are at the top of the page. The page number is at the bottom of the page. This lesson is about word study skills. When you start a lesson, you will find the lesson by its page number. The page number is always at the bottom of the page.

Familiarize the students with the lesson layout and sequence of instruction. Have them locate the Sample item. Explain that you will work through the Sample section together. Then have the students find the STOP sign in the lower right-hand corner of the page.

Book 2 On Your Way to
Scoring High Stanford Achievement Test

Name _____

<table>
<tr><td>Unit 1</td><td>Word Study Skills</td><td>1</td></tr>
<tr><td>My Score</td><td>Lesson</td><td>Page</td></tr>
<tr><td>☐</td><td>1a Word Study Skills ....</td><td>1</td></tr>
<tr><td>☐</td><td>1b Word Study Skills ....</td><td>4</td></tr>
<tr><td>☐</td><td>Test Yourself ....</td><td>6</td></tr>
</table>

<table>
<tr><td>Unit 2</td><td>Reading Vocabulary</td><td>9</td></tr>
<tr><td>My Score</td><td>Lesson</td><td>Page</td></tr>
<tr><td>☐</td><td>2a Vocabulary ....</td><td>9</td></tr>
<tr><td>☐</td><td>2b Vocabulary ....</td><td>11</td></tr>
<tr><td>☐</td><td>Test Yourself ....</td><td>13</td></tr>
</table>

<table>
<tr><td>Unit 3</td><td>Reading Comprehension</td><td>16</td></tr>
<tr><td>My Score</td><td>Lesson</td><td>Page</td></tr>
<tr><td>☐</td><td>3a Comprehension Skills ....</td><td>16</td></tr>
<tr><td>☐</td><td>3b Comprehension Skills ....</td><td>20</td></tr>
<tr><td>☐</td><td>Test Yourself ....</td><td>23</td></tr>
</table>

<table>
<tr><td>Unit 4</td><td>Mathematics Problem Solving</td><td>28</td></tr>
<tr><td>My Score</td><td>Lesson</td><td>Page</td></tr>
<tr><td>☐</td><td>4a Problem Solving ....</td><td>28</td></tr>
<tr><td>☐</td><td>4b Problem Solving ....</td><td>32</td></tr>
<tr><td>☐</td><td>Test Yourself ....</td><td>36</td></tr>
</table>

<table>
<tr><td>Unit 5</td><td>Mathematics Procedures</td><td>42</td></tr>
<tr><td>My Score</td><td>Lesson</td><td>Page</td></tr>
<tr><td>☐</td><td>5a Procedures ....</td><td>42</td></tr>
<tr><td>☐</td><td>5b Procedures ....</td><td>44</td></tr>
<tr><td>☐</td><td>Test Yourself ....</td><td>46</td></tr>
</table>

<table>
<tr><td>Unit 6</td><td>Spelling</td><td>49</td></tr>
<tr><td>My Score</td><td>Lesson</td><td>Page</td></tr>
<tr><td>☐</td><td>6a Spelling Skills ....</td><td>49</td></tr>
<tr><td>☐</td><td>6b Spelling Skills ....</td><td>50</td></tr>
<tr><td>☐</td><td>Test Yourself ....</td><td>51</td></tr>
</table>

iii

Say On some pages, there is a STOP sign. When you see the STOP sign on a page, it means you should stop working. Then we will either do different items or go over the answers to the items you have already completed. I will also explain anything that you did not understand. On other pages, there is a GO sign. When you see the GO sign on a page, it means you should turn the page and continue working.

Have the students locate the Tip sign below Sample A.

Say What does the sign point out to you? *(the tip)* Each lesson has one or more tips that suggest new ways to work through the items. Tests can be tricky. The tips will tell you what to watch out for. They will help you find the best answer quickly.

Explain to the students that the questions in this book and on an achievement test are also called items. Tell the students that each lesson has some items that they will answer by themselves.

Say Now I'll show you how to fill in the spaces for your answers.

Draw several circles on the board and demonstrate how to fill them in. Explain to the students that they should make dark, heavy marks and fill in the circles completely. Allow volunteers to demonstrate filling in answer circles that you have drawn on the board.

Ask the students to turn to the Test Yourself lesson on page 6 of their books. Tell the students the Test Yourself lessons may seem like real tests, but they are not. The Test Yourself lessons are designed to give them opportunities to apply the skills and tips they have learned in timed, trial-run situations. Explain that you will go over the answers together after the students complete each lesson. Then they will figure out their scores and record the number of correct answers in the boxes on the progress chart. Be sure to point out that the students' scores are only for them to see how well they are doing.

Say Each lesson will teach you new skills and tips. What will you have learned when you finish this book? *(word study, reading, mathematics, spelling, language, and listening skills; how to do my best on an achievement test)* When you know you can do your best, how do you think you will feel on test day? You may be a little nervous, but you should also feel confident that you are ready to do your best.

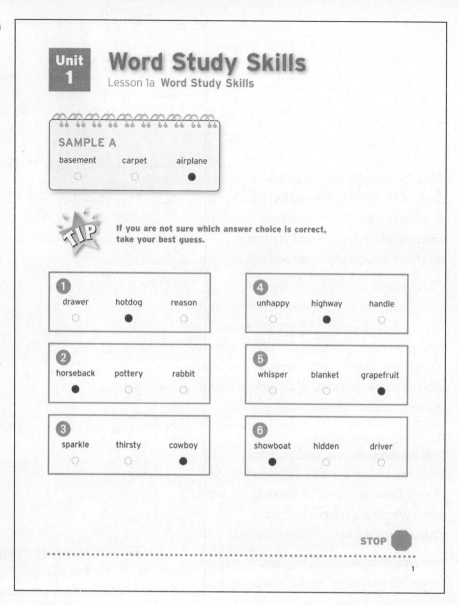

Background

This unit contains three lessons that deal with word study skills. Students answer a variety of questions covering compound words, word structure, contractions, and letter sounds.

• **In Lesson 1a,** students identify compound words, words with suffixes, and contractions. Students are encouraged to follow oral directions, follow complex directions, and take the best guess when unsure of the answer. They subvocalize answer choices and analyze answer choices.

• **In Lesson 1b,** students identify words with matching sounds. Students review the skills introduced in Lesson 1a, work methodically, and gain practice understanding unusual item formats.

• **In the Test Yourself lesson,** the word study and test-taking skills introduced and used in Lessons 1a and 1b are reinforced and presented in a format that gives students the experience of taking an achievement test.

Instructional Objectives

Lesson 1a	**Word Study Skills**	Given three words, students identify which word is a compound word.
		Given three words with the same root and different suffixes, students identify which word is the same as an orally presented word.
		Given three contractions, students identify which contraction has the same meaning as two orally presented words.
Lesson 1b	**Word Study Skills**	Given three words, students identify which word contains the same phoneme as a target word.
	Test Yourself	Given questions similar to those in Lessons 1a and 1b, students utilize word study skills and test-taking strategies on achievement-test formats.

Focus

Word Study Skills
- identifying compound words
- recognizing suffixes
- recognizing contractions

Test-taking Skills
- following oral directions
- following complex directions
- taking the best guess when unsure of the answer
- subvocalizing answer choices
- analyzing answer choices

Sample A

Say Turn to Lesson 1a on page 1. The page number is at the bottom of the page on the right.

Check to see that the students have found the right page.

Say This lesson will give you a chance to show how well you can read different kinds of words. Let's do Sample A. It is in the box near the top of the page. Read the words to yourself as I read them aloud— *basement ... carpet ... airplane.* Which of the words has two words in it? *(pause)* The third answer, *airplane,* contains two words, *air* and *plane.* Fill in the space under *airplane* with a dark mark. Press your pencil firmly so your mark comes out dark. Do you have any questions about what you should do in this part of the lesson?

Check to see that the students have filled in the right answer space. Answer any questions the students have.

⭐TIP

Say Now let's look at the tip.

Read the tip aloud to the students.

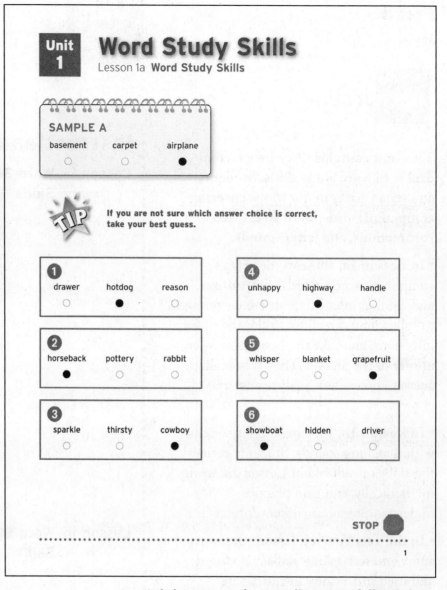

Unit 1 **Word Study Skills**

Lesson 1a **Word Study Skills**

SAMPLE A

basement   carpet   airplane
  ○   ○   ●

TIP If you are not sure which answer choice is correct, take your best guess.

1 drawer   hotdog   reason
     ○   ●   ○

2 horseback pottery rabbit
      ●   ○   ○

3 sparkle   thirsty   cowboy
     ○   ○   ●

4 unhappy highway handle
     ○   ●   ○

5 whisper   blanket   grapefruit
     ○   ○   ●

6 showboat hidden driver
      ●   ○   ○

STOP

1

Say It is important that you listen carefully to the directions and then look at all the answer choices carefully. Think about what you are supposed to do and choose the answer you think is correct. You may find it helpful to say each of the answer choices to yourself while you look at it. If you are not sure which answer choice is correct, take your best guess. It is better to guess than to leave an answer blank.

Practice

Say Now you will do some items just as you did Sample A. For the items on this page, fill in the space under the word that has two words in it. Only do the items on this page. Fill in your answer spaces with dark marks and completely erase any marks for answers that you change. Start working now.

Allow time for the students to fill in their answers.

Say It's time to stop. You have finished the first part of the lesson. Turn to the next page, page 2.

Check to see that the students have found the right page.

Sample B

Say Now you will do another sample item. Look at Sample B at the top of the page.

Check to see that the students have found Sample B.

Say Look at the three words for Sample B. They are almost the same but have different endings. I will use one of the words in a sentence. You are supposed to find that word. Look at the words in your book and listen to the word I say and the sentence in which I use the word. Which is the word *windy*? It is *windy* today. Which answer is *windy*? (pause) The first word is *windy*, so you should fill in the first answer space. Press your pencil firmly so your mark comes out dark. Be sure to fill in the space completely. Do you have any questions about what you should do in this part of the lesson?

Answer any questions the students have. Pause between items to allow students time to fill in their answers.

Say Now you will do more items like Sample B. Listen carefully to what I say. Fill in the space for the answer you think is correct.

7. Put your finger on Number 7. It is below Sample B. Listen to the word and the sentence in which I use the word. Mark under *describing*. We were *describing* our trip. *Describing*.

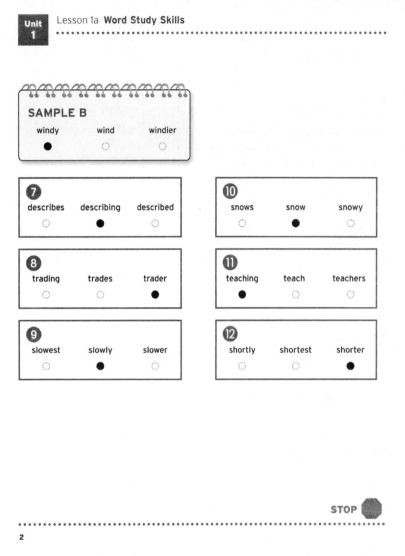

8. Go down to Number 8. Mark under *trader*. A *trader* built this store. *Trader*.

9. Go over to Number 9. *Slowly*. The cow walked *slowly*? *Slowly*.

10. Go down to Number 10. *Snow*. The ground was covered with *snow*. *Snow*.

11. Go down to Number 11. Mark under the word *teaching*. Belinda is *teaching* me how to swim. *Teaching*.

12. Go down to Number 12. Mark under *shorter*. This way is *shorter* than the other way. *Shorter*.

Allow a moment for the students to relax.

Say Look at the next page, page 3.

Check to be sure the students have found the correct page.

Sample C

Say Now you'll do Sample C. It is in the box at the top of the page on the left. The three words are *haven't … hasn't … hadn't.* These words are shortened forms of other words. I will say two words and use them in a sentence. You will find the shortened word that means the same thing. Listen carefully. Which word means *have not?* I *have not* read that book. *Have not. (pause)* The first word, *haven't,* means *have not,* so you should fill in the first answer space. Press your pencil firmly so your mark comes out dark. Be sure to fill in the space completely. Do you have any questions about what you should do in this part of the lesson?

Answer any questions the students have. Allow time between items for the students to fill in their answers.

Say Now you will do more items like Sample C. Listen carefully to what I say. Fill in the space for the answer you think is correct.

13. Put your finger on Number 13. Which answer means *he will?* *He will* be home soon. *He will.*

14. Go down to Number 14. Which one means *were not?* They *were not* on time. *Were not.*

15. Go to Number 15. Which one means *do not?* *Do not* forget your coat. *Do not.*

16. Put your finger on Number 16. Which answer means *should not?* The store *should not* be far from here. *Should not.*

17. Go down to Number 17. Which one means *is not?* My friend *is not* here. *Is not.*

18. Go to Number 18. Which one means *she would?* *She would* like to eat now. *She would.*

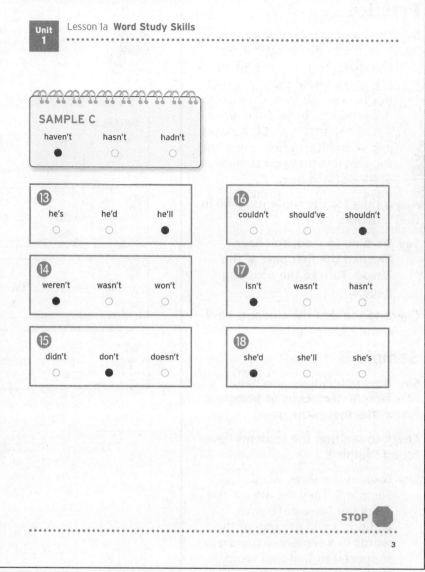

Say It's time to stop. You have finished Lesson 1a.

Review the answers with the students. Ask them if they remembered to look at all the answer choices and take the best guess if they were unsure of the correct answer. If any items caused particular difficulty, work through each of the answer choices.

Have the students indicate completion of the lesson by entering their score for this activity on the progress chart at the beginning of the book. Provide the students whatever help is necessary to record their scores.

Unit 1 Lesson 1b
Word Study Skills

Focus

Word Study Skill
- matching phonemes

Test-taking Skills
- following oral directions
- following complex directions
- working methodically
- subvocalizing answer choices
- understanding unusual item formats

Sample

Say Turn to Lesson 1b on page 4. The page number is at the bottom of the page on the left.

Check to see that the students have found the right page.

Say In this lesson, you will work with word sounds. Find the Sample at the top of the page. The first word you see is *match.* The letter *m* in *match* has a line under it. Now look at the other three words in the box. Which word has the same /m/ sound as *match*? *(pause)* The second answer, *stem,* has the same /m/ sound as *match.* Fill in the space under the word *stem.* Press your pencil firmly so your mark comes out dark. Be sure the space is completely filled in. Do you have any questions?

Check to see that the students have filled in the right answer space.

★**TIP**

Say Now let's look at the tip.

Read the tip aloud to the students.

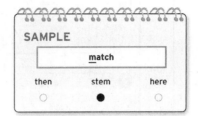

SAMPLE

match

then   stem   here

TIP — Say each word to yourself. Listen for the sound of the underlined part.

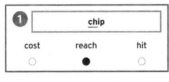

1 chip

cost   reach   hit

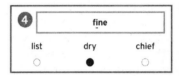

4 fine

list   dry   chief

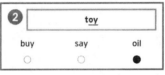

2 toy

buy   say   oil

5 friend

scarf   frost   raft

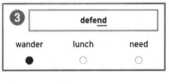

3 defend

wander   lunch   need

GO →

4

Say When you do the items in this lesson, you should say the word with the underlined part to yourself. Listen for the sound made by the underlined part. Then say each of the answer choices to yourself. Choose the one that has the same sound as the underlined part. Remember, the sound may be made by different letters, and it may be in a different part of the word.

Practice

Say Now you will do more items just as you did the Sample. Say the word with the underlined part to yourself. Think about the sound made by the underlined part. Then look at the answer choices. Fill in the space under the answer that has the same sound as the underlined part of the first word. Do you have any questions? Let's begin.

Allow time for the students to fill in their answers. Answer any questions the students have. Encourage the students to say the first word and the answer choices to themselves. They should listen for the answer that has the same sound as the underlined part of the target word. Remind them that the sound does not have to be in the same place in the answer.

Say It's time to stop. You have finished Lesson 1b.

Review the answers with the students. Ask them if they remembered to look at all the answer choices. If any items caused particular difficulty, work through each of the answer choices. Point out instances where the sound in the correct answer was made by letters other than those underlined in the first word.

Have the students indicate completion of the lesson by entering their score for this activity on the progress chart at the beginning of the book. Provide the students whatever help is necessary to record their scores.

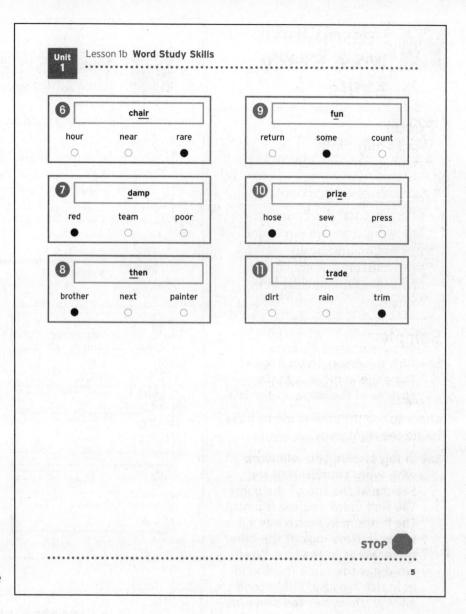

Unit 1 Test Yourself: Word Study Skills

Focus

Word Study Skills
- identifying compound words
- recognizing suffixes
- recognizing contractions
- matching phonemes

Test-taking Skills
- following oral directions
- following complex directions
- taking the best guess when unsure of the answer
- subvocalizing answer choices
- analyzing answer choices
- working methodically
- understanding unusual item formats

This lesson simulates an actual test-taking experience. Therefore, it is recommended that the directions be read verbatim and the suggested procedures be followed.

Directions

Administration Time: approximately 25 minutes

Say Turn to the Test Yourself lesson on page 6.

Check to be sure the students have found the right page. Point out to the students that this Test Yourself lesson is like a real test, but that they will score it themselves to see how well they are doing. Explain that it is important to answer as many questions as possible. Remind the students to listen carefully and to take the best guess when they are unsure of the answer.

Say This lesson will check how well you remember what you learned in other lessons. Be sure your answer spaces are completely filled in. Press your pencil firmly so that your marks come out dark. Completely erase any marks for answers that you change. Do not write anything except your answers in your book.

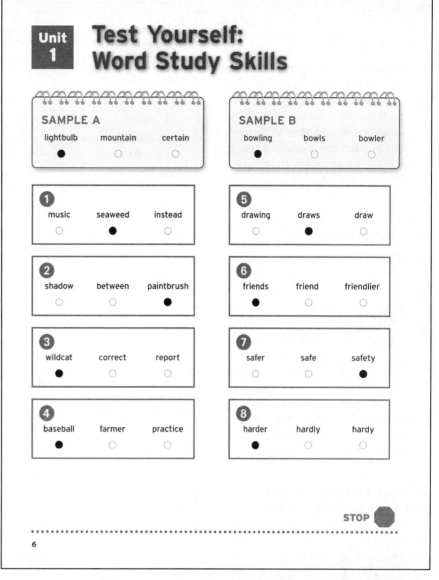

Find Sample A in the box near the top of the page. Read the words to yourself as I read them aloud. *lightbulb ... mountain ... certain.* Which of the words has two words in it? Mark the space for your answer.

Allow time for the students to fill in their answers.

Say You should have filled in the space under the first answer, *lightbulb.* If you chose another answer, erase yours and fill in the first answer space now.

Check to see that the students have marked the correct space.

Say Now you will do some more items just as you did Sample A. For Numbers 1 through 4, read the three words. Fill in the space under the word that has two words in it. Only do Numbers 1 through 4. You will do the other items later. Fill in your answer spaces with dark marks and completely erase any marks for answers that you change. Do you have any questions? Start working now.

Allow enough time for the students to do Numbers 1 through 4.

Say Now you will do Sample B. It is at the top of the page on the right. Look at the three words. They are almost the same but have different endings. I will use one of the words in a sentence. You are supposed to find that word. Look at the words in your book and listen to the word I say and the sentence in which I use the word. Fill in the space under the word *bowling*. We went *bowling* yesterday. *Bowling.*

Allow time for the students to fill in their answers.

Say You should have filled in the first answer. If you chose another answer, erase yours and fill in the first space now.

Check to see that the students have marked the correct space.

Say Now you will do more items like Sample B. Listen carefully to what I say. Fill in the space for the answer you think is correct.

Allow time between items for the students to fill in their answers.

5. Move down to Number 5. *Draws.* Nancy *draws* well. *Draws.*

6. Move down to Number 6. Mark under *friends.* My *friends* are here. *Friends.*

7. Move down to Number 7. Mark under *safety.* We learned about *safety* today. *Safety.*

8. Go to the last row. *Harder.* This puzzle is *harder* than the other one. *Harder.*

Allow a moment for the students to relax.

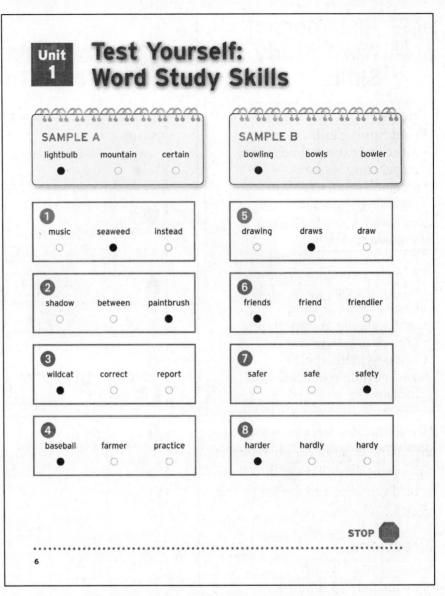

Say Look at the next page, page 7.

Check to be sure the students have found the correct page.

Say Now you will do Sample C. It is in the box at the top of the page. The three words are *wasn't … isn't … can't.* These words are shortened forms of other words. I will say two words and then use them in a sentence. Listen carefully. *Can not.* My sister *can not* come with us. Fill in the space under the word that means the same as *can not.*

Allow time for the students to fill in their answers.

Say The last answer is correct. If you chose another answer, erase yours and fill in the space under the last answer now.

Check to see that the students have marked the correct space.

Say Now you will do more items like Sample C. Listen carefully to what I say. Fill in the space for the answer you think is correct.

Allow time between items for the students to fill in their answers.

9.   Put your finger on Number 9 under Sample C. Which answer means *where is? Where is* my coat? *Where is.*

10. Move down to Number 10. Which word means *has not? The bus has not arrived yet. Has not.*

11. Go to Number 11. Which answer means *he would? He would* come if you asked him. *He would.*

12. Go up to Number 12. Which answer means *are not?* Our windows *are not* open. *Are not.*

Allow a moment for the students to relax.

Say Find Sample D in the middle of the page. The first word you see is *best.* The letter *b* in *best* has a line under it. Now look at the other three words in the box. Mark the space under the word that has the same /b/ sound as *best.*

Allow time for the students to fill in their answers.

Say The second answer, *band,* is correct. If you chose another answer, erase yours and fill in the space under *band* now.

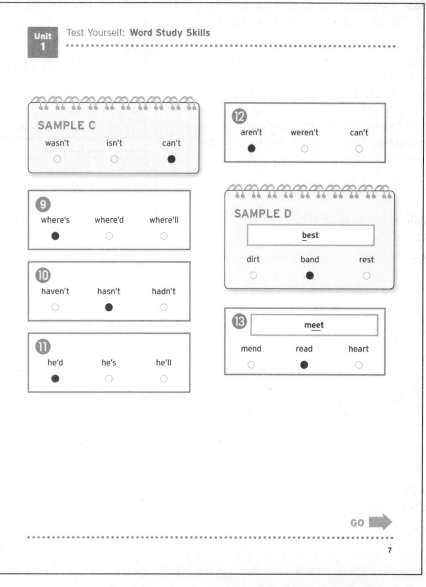

SAMPLE C

wasn't   isn't   can't

9   where's   where'd   where'll

10   haven't   hasn't   hadn't

11   he'd   he's   he'll

12   aren't   weren't   can't

SAMPLE D

best

dirt   band   rest

13   meet

mend   read   heart

GO

7

Check to see that the students have correctly filled in their answer spaces with a dark mark.

Say Now you will do more items just as you did Sample D. Say the word with the underlined part to yourself. Think about the sound made by the underlined part. Then look at the answer choices. Fill in the space under the answer that has the same sound as the underlined part of the first word. If you are not sure which answer is correct, take your best guess. Fill in your answer spaces with dark marks. When you come to the GO sign at the bottom of the page, go on to the next page and continue working. Work until you come to the STOP sign at the bottom of page 8. Completely erase any marks for answers that you change. Do you have any questions? Start working now.

Allow time for the students to fill in their answers.

Say It's time to stop. You have finished the Test Yourself lesson.

Review the answers with the students. Have the students indicate completion of the lesson by entering their score for this activity on the progress chart at the beginning of the book. Provide the students whatever help is necessary to record their scores.

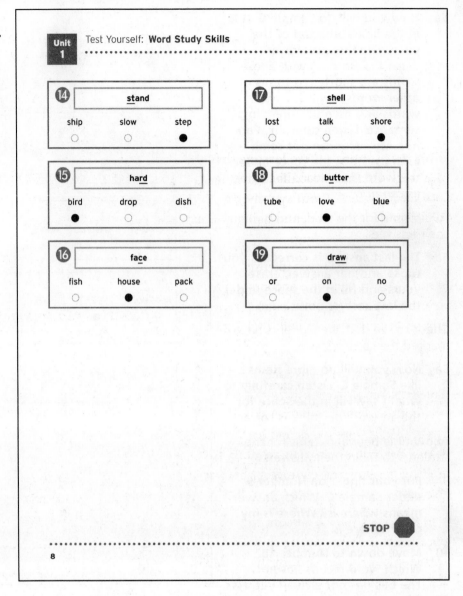

Background

This unit contains three lessons that deal with vocabulary skills. Students answer questions about synonyms, multi-meaning words, and using context to derive word meaning.

• **In Lesson 2a,** students identify synonyms. Students are encouraged to follow printed directions, consider every answer choice, skip difficult items, and work methodically.

• **In Lesson 2b,** students identify multi-meaning words and words in context. Students review the skills introduced in Lesson 2a and learn about taking the best guess, using context to find the answer, and comparing answer choices.

• **In the Test Yourself lesson,** the vocabulary and test-taking skills introduced and used in Lessons 2a and 2b are reinforced and presented in a format that gives students the experience of taking an achievement test.

Instructional Objectives

Lesson 2a Vocabulary	Given a phrase with an underlined word, students identify which of four answer choices means the same as the underlined word.
Lesson 2b Vocabulary	Given a sentence with an underlined word, students identify which of four sentences uses the underlined word in the same way. Given a sentence with an underlined word, students use the context of the sentence to identify which of four answer choices means the same as the underlined word.
Test Yourself	Given questions similar to those in Lessons 2a and 2b, students utilize vocabulary skills and test-taking strategies on achievement-test formats.

Unit 2 Lesson 2a Vocabulary

Focus

Vocabulary Skill
• identifying synonyms

Test-taking Skills
• following printed directions
• considering every answer choice
• skipping difficult items and returning to them later
• working methodically

Samples A and B

Say Turn to Lesson 2a on page 9. The page number is at the bottom of the page on the right.

Check to see that the students have found the right page.

Say In this lesson, you will show how well you understand different kinds of vocabulary words. Let's do Sample A. It is in the box at the top of the page. Read the item to yourself as I read it out loud. *To listen is to— see … feel … hear … think.* Which of the four answers means about the same as the underlined word? *(pause) Hear* is correct. *Listen* and *hear* mean about the same thing. Fill in the space beside the word *hear.* Be sure your answer space is completely filled in with a dark mark.

Check to see that the students have filled in the right answer space.

Say Now do Sample B yourself. It is in the box at the top of the page. Read the item to yourself. Which of the four answers means about the same as the underlined word? *(pause)* The correct answer is *quiet.* Fill in the space beside the word *quiet.* Be sure your answer space is completely filled in with a dark mark.

Check to see that the students have filled in the right answer space.

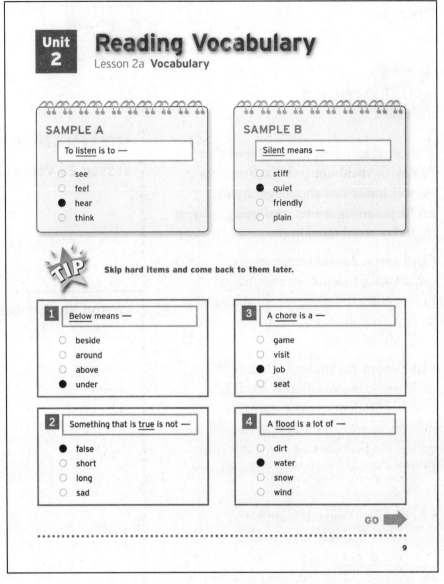

Unit 2 Reading Vocabulary
Lesson 2a Vocabulary

SAMPLE A

To listen is to —

○ see
○ feel
● hear
○ think

SAMPLE B

Silent means —

○ stiff
● quiet
○ friendly
○ plain

TIP Skip hard items and come back to them later.

1 Below means —

○ beside
○ around
○ above
● under

3 A chore is a —

○ game
○ visit
● job
○ seat

2 Something that is true is not —

● false
○ short
○ long
○ sad

4 A flood is a lot of —

○ dirt
● water
○ snow
○ wind

GO

9

TIP

Say Now let's look at the tip.

Read the tip aloud to the students.

Say Sometimes you won't know the right answer right away. When this happens, skip the item and move on to the next one. After you have tried all the other items, come back to the ones you skipped.

Be sure students understand how to skip items. Elaborate as necessary so students understand that they should come back to items they skipped.

Practice

Say Now you will do some items yourself. It's a good idea to double-check to be sure that you have filled in the space for the answer choice you think is correct. If you make a mistake when you fill in the answer space, your answer will still be counted wrong, even if you knew what the correct answer was. When you come to the GO sign at the bottom of the page, go on to the next page and continue working. Work until you come to the STOP sign at the bottom of page 10. Fill in your answer spaces with dark marks and completely erase any marks for answers that you change. Do you have any questions? Start working now.

Allow time for the students to fill in their answers.

Say It's time to stop. You have finished Lesson 2a.

Review the answers with the students. If any items caused particular difficulty, work through each of the answer choices. Have volunteers identify any items they skipped.

Have the students indicate completion of the lesson by entering their score for this activity on the progress chart at the beginning of the book. Provide the students whatever help is necessary to record their scores.

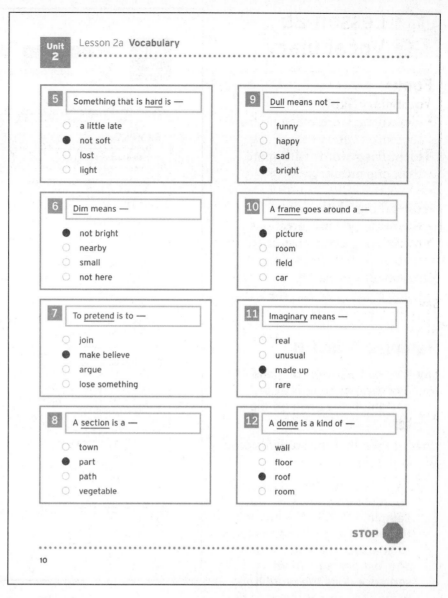

Unit 2 — Lesson 2a Vocabulary

5 Something that is <u>hard</u> is —
- ○ a little late
- ● not soft
- ○ lost
- ○ light

6 <u>Dim</u> means —
- ● not bright
- ○ nearby
- ○ small
- ○ not here

7 To <u>pretend</u> is to —
- ○ join
- ● make believe
- ○ argue
- ○ lose something

8 A <u>section</u> is a —
- ○ town
- ● part
- ○ path
- ○ vegetable

9 <u>Dull</u> means not —
- ○ funny
- ○ happy
- ○ sad
- ● bright

10 A <u>frame</u> goes around a —
- ● picture
- ○ room
- ○ field
- ○ car

11 <u>Imaginary</u> means —
- ○ real
- ○ unusual
- ● made up
- ○ rare

12 A <u>dome</u> is a kind of —
- ○ wall
- ○ floor
- ● roof
- ○ room

STOP

10

Focus

Vocabulary Skills
- identifying word meaning from sentence context
- identifying words with more than one meaning

Test-taking Skills
- following printed directions
- considering every answer choice
- taking the best guess when unsure of the answer
- using context to find the answer
- comparing answer choices

Samples A and B

Say Turn to Lesson 2b on page 11. The page number is at the bottom of the page on the right.

Check to see that the students have found the right page.

Say This is another lesson about vocabulary words. Let's do Sample A. It is in the box at the top of the page. Read the item to yourself as I read it aloud. *She lost her ring.* In which sentence does the word *ring* mean the same thing as in the sentence above? The answers are: *A glass can be made to ring. … We joined hands to form a ring. … Did you ring the doorbell? … A ring was on her finger.* (pause) The last answer is correct. Fill in the space beside the last answer. Make sure your circle is completely filled in with a dark mark.

Check to see that the students have filled in the right answer space. Explain the meaning of *ring* in each sentence. Discuss why the last answer is better than the other choices.

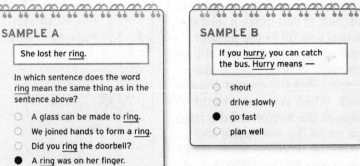

Reading Vocabulary
Unit 2 — Lesson 2b Vocabulary

SAMPLE A

> She lost her ring.

In which sentence does the word ring mean the same thing as in the sentence above?

- ○ A glass can be made to ring.
- ○ We joined hands to form a ring.
- ○ Did you ring the doorbell?
- ● A ring was on her finger.

SAMPLE B

> If you hurry, you can catch the bus. Hurry means —

- ○ shout
- ○ drive slowly
- ● go fast
- ○ plan well

Use the meaning of the sentence to find the right answer.

1
> Pick up your clothes.

In which sentence does the word pick mean the same thing as in the sentence above?

- ○ Use a pick to break up the dirt.
- ○ This apple is the pick of the crop.
- ● Jay volunteered to pick up trash.
- ○ We'll pick you up at noon.

2
> Be sure to tie the knot tightly.

In which sentence does the word tie mean the same thing as in the sentence above?

- ● Tie the string around the papers.
- ○ This tie goes with that shirt.
- ○ The game ended in a tie.
- ○ We used a railroad tie for a step.

GO ➡

11

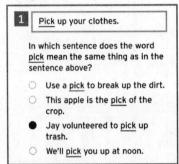

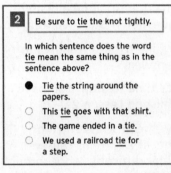

Say Now we'll do Sample B. Read the item to yourself while I read it aloud. *If you hurry, you can catch the bus. Hurry means—shout … drive slowly … go fast … plan well.* Which of the four answers is correct? (pause) The third answer, *go fast,* is correct. Fill in the space beside the third answer. Be sure your answer space is completely filled in with a dark mark.

Check to see that the students have filled in the right answer space.

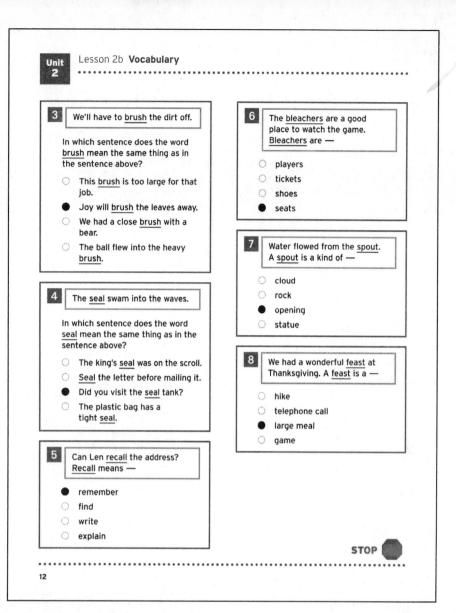

★TIP

Say Now let's look at the tip.

Have a volunteer read the tip aloud.

Say In this lesson, you should use the meaning of each sentence to find the right answer. Begin by reading the whole item. Think about what each sentence means. Then look at each answer choice. Compare the answer choices with one another. Choose the answer that makes the most sense.

Practice

Say Now you will do more items. Read each item carefully because there are two kinds of items in this lesson. Look at all the answer choices and choose the one that makes the most sense. When you come to the GO sign at the bottom of the page, go on to the next page and continue working. Work until you come to the STOP sign at the bottom of the next page. Fill in your answer spaces with dark marks and completely erase any marks for answers that you change. Do you have any questions? Start working now.

Allow time for the students to fill in their answers.

Say It's time to stop. You have finished Lesson 2b.

Review the answers with the students. If any items caused particular difficulty, explain thoroughly why the correct answer is right and the other choices are wrong. If necessary, review the importance of using sentence context to find the answer.

Have the students indicate completion of the lesson by entering their score for this activity on the progress chart at the beginning of the book. Provide the students whatever help is necessary to record their scores.

The detail within the image shows a student worksheet page:

Unit 2 — Lesson 2b Vocabulary

3 We'll have to brush the dirt off.

In which sentence does the word brush mean the same thing as in the sentence above?

○ This brush is too large for that job.
● Joy will brush the leaves away.
○ We had a close brush with a bear.
○ The ball flew into the heavy brush.

4 The seal swam into the waves.

In which sentence does the word seal mean the same thing as in the sentence above?

○ The king's seal was on the scroll.
○ Seal the letter before mailing it.
● Did you visit the seal tank?
○ The plastic bag has a tight seal.

5 Can Len recall the address? Recall means —

● remember
○ find
○ write
○ explain

6 The bleachers are a good place to watch the game. Bleachers are —

○ players
○ tickets
○ shoes
● seats

7 Water flowed from the spout. A spout is a kind of —

○ cloud
○ rock
● opening
○ statue

8 We had a wonderful feast at Thanksgiving. A feast is a —

○ hike
○ telephone call
● large meal
○ game

STOP

12

Focus

Vocabulary Skills
- identifying synonyms
- identifying word meaning from sentence context
- identifying words with more than one meaning

Test-taking Skills
- following printed directions
- considering every answer choice
- skipping difficult items and returning to them later
- working methodically
- taking the best guess when unsure of the answer
- using context to find the answer
- comparing answer choices

This lesson simulates an actual test-taking experience. Therefore, it is recommended that the directions be read verbatim and the suggested procedures be followed.

Directions

Administration Time: approximately 25 minutes

Say Turn to the Test Yourself lesson on page 13.

Check to be sure the students have found the right page. Point out to the students that this Test Yourself lesson is like a real test, but that they will score it themselves to see how well they are doing. Explain that it is important to answer as many questions as possible. Remind the students to listen carefully and to take the best guess when they are unsure of the answer.

Say This lesson will check how well you remember what you practiced in other lessons. Be sure your answer spaces are completely filled in. Press your pencil firmly so that your marks come out dark. Completely erase any marks for answers that you change. Do not write anything except your answers in your book.

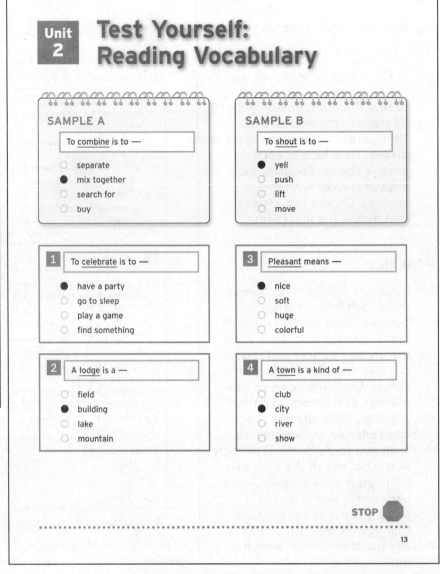

Unit 2 — Test Yourself: Reading Vocabulary

SAMPLE A

To combine is to —
- ○ separate
- ● mix together
- ○ search for
- ○ buy

SAMPLE B

To shout is to —
- ● yell
- ○ push
- ○ lift
- ○ move

1 To celebrate is to —
- ● have a party
- ○ go to sleep
- ○ play a game
- ○ find something

3 Pleasant means —
- ● nice
- ○ soft
- ○ huge
- ○ colorful

2 A lodge is a —
- ○ field
- ● building
- ○ lake
- ○ mountain

4 A town is a kind of —
- ○ club
- ● city
- ○ river
- ○ show

STOP

13

Say Find Sample A in the box at the top of the page. Read Sample A to yourself as I read it aloud. *To __combine__ is to—separate ... mix together ... search for ... buy.* Which of the four answers means about the same as the underlined word? Mark the space for your answer.

Allow time for the students to fill in their answers.

Say You should have filled in the second answer, *mix together.* If you chose another answer, erase yours and fill in the second answer now.

Check to see that the students have marked the correct space.

Say Now do Sample B. Read the item to yourself. Which of the four answers means about the same as the underlined word? Mark the space for your answer.

Allow time for the students to fill in their answers.

Say You should have filled in the space beside *yell*. If you chose another answer, erase yours and fill in the first answer space now.

Check to see that the students have marked the correct space.

Say Now you will do some more items like the samples. Work until you come to the STOP sign at the bottom of the page. Fill in your answer spaces with dark marks and completely erase any marks for answers that you change. Do you have any questions? Start working now.

Allow time for the students to fill in their answers. Walk around the room and provide the students with any help they need.

Say It's time to stop. You have finished the first part of the lesson. Turn to the next page, page 14.

Check to see that the students have found the right page.

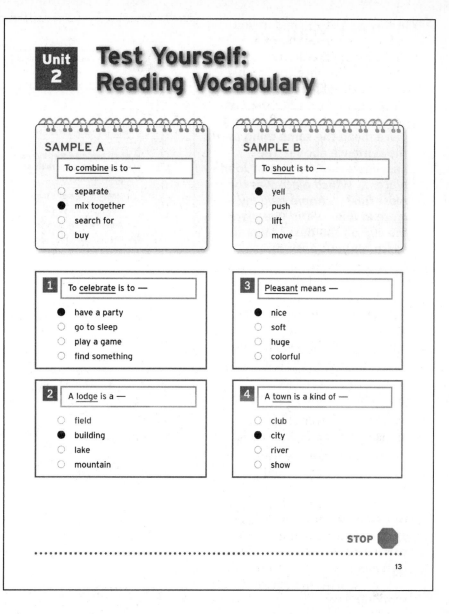

Unit 2 Test Yourself: Reading Vocabulary

SAMPLE A

To <u>combine</u> is to —
○ separate
● mix together
○ search for
○ buy

SAMPLE B

To <u>shout</u> is to —
● yell
○ push
○ lift
○ move

1 To <u>celebrate</u> is to —
● have a party
○ go to sleep
○ play a game
○ find something

2 A <u>lodge</u> is a —
○ field
● building
○ lake
○ mountain

3 <u>Pleasant</u> means —
● nice
○ soft
○ huge
○ colorful

4 A <u>town</u> is a kind of —
○ club
● city
○ river
○ show

STOP

13

Say In this part of the lesson you will use the meaning of a sentence to identify words. Read the sentence for Sample C to yourself while I read it aloud. *Place the book on the shelf.* In which sentence does the word *place* mean the same thing as in the sentence above? The answers are—*Meet me at John's place.* ... *Which place was the most fun? ... Annie held my place in line. ... Did you place the cup on the desk?* Mark the space for your answer.

Allow time for the students to fill in their answers.

Say You should have filled in the last answer space. If you chose another answer, erase yours and fill in the last answer space now.

Check to see that the students have marked the correct space.

Say Now you will do some more items. Complete the items on this page just as we did Sample C. Work until you come to the STOP sign at the bottom of the page. Fill in your answer spaces with dark marks and completely erase any marks for answers that you change. Do you have any questions? Start working now.

Allow time for the students to fill in their answers.

Say It's time to stop. You have finished this part of the lesson. Turn to the next page, page 15.

Check to see that the students have found the right page.

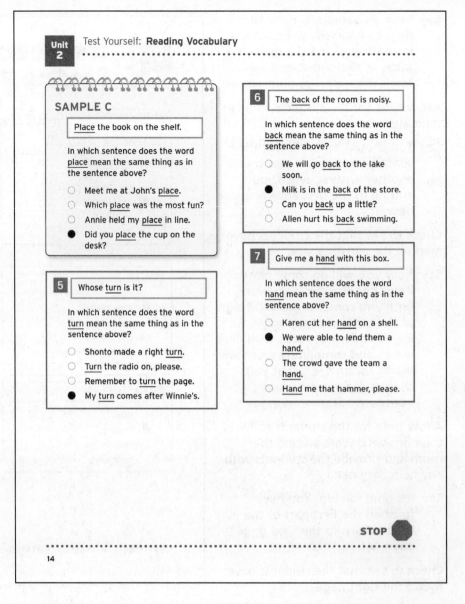

Say Now we'll do Sample D. Read it to yourself as I read it aloud: *My arm was <u>aching</u> after I bumped it. <u>Aching</u> means— sore … weak … strong … wet.* Which answer is correct? Mark the space for your answer.

Allow time for the students to fill in their answers.

Say You should have filled in the space beside the first answer, *sore*. If you chose another answer, erase yours and fill in the first answer space now.

Check to see that the students have marked the correct space.

Say Now you will do some more items. Complete the items on this page just as we did Sample D. Work until you come to the STOP sign at the bottom of the page. Fill in your answer spaces with dark marks and completely erase any marks for answers that you change. Do you have any questions? Start working now.

Allow time for the students to fill in their answers.

Say It's time to stop. You have completed the Test Yourself lesson.

Review the answers with the students. Have the students indicate completion of the lesson by entering their score for this activity on the progress chart at the beginning of the book. Provide the students whatever help is necessary to record their scores.

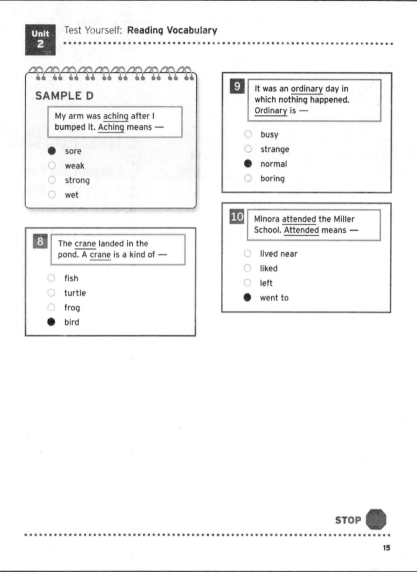

Background

This unit contains three lessons that deal with reading comprehension skills. Students read passages and answer a variety of questions about what they have read.

• **In Lessons 3a and 3b,** students read a passage and answer questions based on the content of the passage. Students learn to skim a passage, refer to a passage to answer questions, and use key words. They work methodically, reread questions, and reason from facts and evidence.

• **In the Test Yourself lesson,** the reading comprehension and test-taking skills introduced and used in Lessons 3a and 3b are reinforced and presented in a format that gives students the experience of taking an achievement test.

Instructional Objectives

Lesson 3a **Comprehension Skills** Lesson 3b **Comprehension Skills**	Given a written passage and a literal or inferential question based on the passage, students identify which of four answer choices is correct.
Test Yourself	Given questions similar to those in Lessons 3a and 3b, students utilize reading comprehension skills and test-taking strategies on achievement-test formats.

Lesson 3a
Comprehension Skills

Focus

Reading Skills
- recognizing details
- drawing conclusions
- recognizing the author's purpose
- identifying informational resources
- understanding the main idea
- making inferences

Test-taking Skills
- skimming a passage
- referring to a passage to answer questions
- identifying and using key words to find the answer
- working methodically

Samples A and B

Say Turn to Lesson 3a on page 16. The page number is at the bottom of the page on the left.

Check to see that the students have found the right page.

Say In this lesson, you will answer questions about stories that you read. Find Sample A at the top of the page. Read the story to yourself. *(pause)* Now read the question to yourself while I read it aloud. *Which of these must be decided before the first meeting? Is it—Who will run the club? … What will the club be named? … Where will the meeting be held? … Who will be invited to join the club?* To find the correct answer, look back at the story. Which answer is correct? *(Where will the meeting be held?)* Fill in the space beside the third answer. Make sure the space is completely filled in. Press your pencil firmly so that your mark comes out dark.

Check to see that the students have filled in the right answer space.

SAMPLES

Kids' Club

You and your friends can start your own club. Clubs can do things for fun. Clubs can also help others. These are some of the things you and your friends should think of before you start your club.

1. What will be the name of the club?
2. What is the purpose of the club? What will we want this club to do?
3. Who will run the club?
4. Who can join the club?
5. How will decisions be made?
6. When will we meet?
7. Where will we have our meetings?

SAMPLE A

Which of these must be decided before the first meeting?

- ○ Who will run the club?
- ○ What will the club be named?
- ● Where will the meeting be held?
- ○ Who will be invited to join the club?

SAMPLE B

This list will help you —

- ○ play a new game
- ● start a new club
- ○ do well in school
- ○ become a member of a team

"Skim" the story. Look back at the story to answer the questions. You don't have to memorize the story.

GO

16

Say Do Sample B yourself. Read the question and the answer choices. Look back at the story to find the answer. Which answer is correct? *(pause)* The second answer, *start a new club,* is correct. Fill in the space beside the second answer. Make sure the space is completely filled in. Press your pencil firmly so that your mark comes out dark.

Check to see that the students have filled in the right answer space.

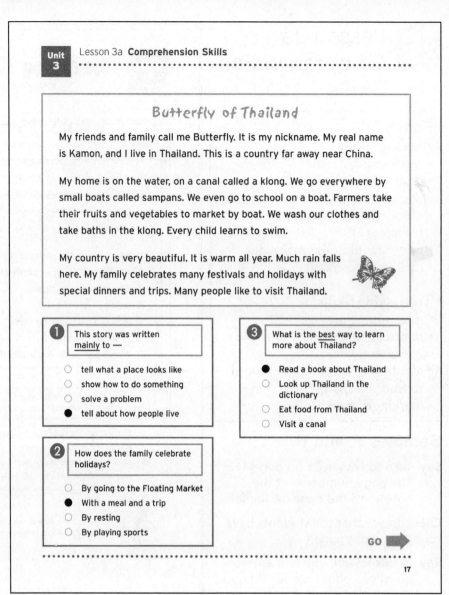

★**TIP**

Say Now let's look at the tip.

Read the tip aloud to the students.

Say Whenever you answer questions about a reading passage, begin by *skimming* the passage. This means you should read it quickly just to get an idea of what it is about. You don't have to memorize the story. Then, when you do the items, read the questions and look back to the story to answer them. You don't have to reread the story for each question. Instead, just look for important words in the question. They will tell you where in the story to look for the correct answer. If you can find the same important words in the story, you can usually find the correct answer nearby.

Use the sample items to demonstrate how to refer back to the passage using key words.

Say Look at the next page, page 17.

Check to be sure the students have found the right page.

Practice

Say Now you will do more items. Skim the stories then read the questions and answer them in the same way that we did the samples. Fill in your answer spaces with dark marks. When you see a GO sign at the bottom of a page, turn the page and continue working. Work until you come to the STOP sign at the bottom of page 19. Completely erase any marks for answers that you change. Do you have any questions? Start working now.

Allow time for the students to fill in their answers. Walk around the room and encourage the students to refer to the passage when they choose their answers.

Lost and Found

Bud's pet was a tiny, yellow bird named Emma. Every day he would open the door to Emma's cage and hold out his finger. The bird liked to hop on Bud's finger. She would turn her head to the side and look at him and say, "Tweet, tweet." She seemed to know that Bud was her friend.

Bud gave Emma seeds in a cup. He put pieces of apple in her cage. He gave her a long, white bone to sharpen her beak. He put some gravel in a cup for Emma. He made sure she had fresh water every day. At night he put a blanket over her cage. Sometimes Bud let Emma fly around the house.

One day, Emma was out of her cage flying around the house. Bud was cleaning the cage and putting in fresh seeds and water. Bud's brother opened the door to the house and forgot to close it. Emma flew outside before Bud could catch her.

"I am so sorry, Bud. I did not know Emma was out of the cage. I will help you find her," Bud's brother said.

The boys went all over the neighborhood. They called and called. They asked all the people if anyone had seen the little, yellow bird that said, "Tweet, tweet." No one had seen her.

The boys were very sad. Bud wanted to cry, but he did not. He thought he would never see his bird again.

GO ➡

Say It's time to stop. You have finished Lesson 3a.

Review the answers with the students. If any questions caused particular difficulty, work through the stories, questions, and answer choices. Have volunteers explain how they decided which answer choices were correct.

Have the students indicate completion of the lesson by entering their score for this activity on the progress chart at the beginning of the book. Provide the students whatever help is necessary to record their scores.

Lesson 3a **Comprehension Skills**

The next morning, their mother opened the door to get the newspaper. There, sitting on a bush, was Emma! "Bud, come here quickly," she called.

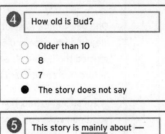 Bud put out his finger just as he did when he was taking Emma out of her cage. She hopped on his finger and let him carry her back into the house. She said "Tweet, tweet" and seemed very happy to be home.

All day long, Bud had a big smile on his face. In the future, he would always be extra careful whenever he cleaned Emma's cage.

4 How old is Bud?

○ Older than 10
○ 8
○ 7
● The story does not say

5 This story is mainly about —

● a boy and his bird
○ a boy who did something wrong
○ learning to care for a pet
○ searching but not finding

6 Why did Bud's mother call him when she saw the bird?

○ She did not know what to do to get the bird back.
○ She thought his brother might scare the bird away.
● She thought Bud could catch Emma.
○ She was afraid the cat might get the bird.

STOP

19

Unit 3 Lesson 3b
Comprehension Skills

Focus

Reading Skills
- deriving word or phrase meaning
- recognizing details
- recognizing the author's purpose
- understanding sequence
- making predictions
- choosing the best title for a story

Test-taking Skills
- skimming a passage
- referring to a passage to answer questions
- working methodically
- rereading questions
- reasoning from facts and evidence

Samples A and B

Say Turn to Lesson 3b on page 20. The page number is at the bottom of the page on the left.

Check to see that the students have found the right page.

Say In this lesson, you will answer more questions about stories that you read. Let's begin by doing Sample A. Find Sample A at the top of the page. Read the story to yourself. *(pause)* Now read the question to yourself while I read it aloud. *What are most bandages made of today?* The answers are— *Cloth … Plastic … Cotton … Paper.* Which answer is correct? *(pause)* The second answer, *Plastic,* is correct. Fill in the space beside the second answer. Press your pencil firmly so that your mark comes out dark.

Check to see that the students have filled in the right answer space.

SAMPLES

How Bandages Are Made

One of the best first-aid treatments is a bandage. A bandage will help a cut heal faster. It will also keep the cut clean and prevent infection.

Long ago, bandages were just strips of cloth. Later, people made the cloth sticky. Finally, pads were added to the sticky strips of cloth.

Today, most bandages are made of plastic. A special glue is put on the plastic, then it is cut into strips. Gauze pads are attached to the sticky side of the plastic. The gauze keeps the glue off the cut and protects it. As part of the process, bandages are put into a giant oven. They are heated to kill any germs on them. This means you can put a bandage on a cut and feel safe.

SAMPLE A

What are most bandages made of today?

○ Cloth
● Plastic
○ Cotton
○ Paper

SAMPLE B

This story was written <u>mainly</u> to tell you —

○ when you should use a bandage
○ where you can buy bandages
● how bandages are made
○ how to give first aid

GO ➡

20

Say Do Sample B yourself. Read the question and the answer choices. Look back at the story to find the answer. Which answer is correct? *(how bandages are made)* The third answer, *how bandages are made,* is correct. Fill in the space beside the third answer. Make sure the space is completely filled in. Press your pencil firmly so that your mark comes out dark.

Check to see that the students have filled in the right answer space.

Say If you are not sure you understand a question, read both the question and answer choices twice. This will help you understand the question better. Don't worry about wasting time. There is no time limit on this lesson. If you think it will help, take your time and read the question and the answer choices twice.

Turn to the next page, page 21.

Check to be sure the students have found the right page.

Practice

Say Now you will do more items. Read the stories and then answer the questions in the same way that we did the samples. Use important words in the question to find the answer. Sometimes the answer will be stated in the story, but other times you will have to read between the lines to find the answer. Look back at the story to answer the questions. When you see the GO sign at the bottom of the page, go on to the next page and continue working. Work until you come to the STOP sign at the bottom of page 22. Completely erase any marks for answers that you change. Do you have any questions? Start working now.

Allow time for the students to fill in their answers. Walk around the room and encourage the students to eliminate answer choices they know are wrong.

 Unit 3 Lesson 3b **Comprehension Skills**

Brave Tonga

Tonga was a furry, golden lion cub. He loved to run and play all day. When night came, Tonga stayed as close as he could to his mother. "I'm afraid of the dark, Mama. Stay right here by me, Mama," Tonga said every night.

When he got bigger, Tonga's mother talked to him about being afraid. She said that lions were brave. "Lions are not afraid of anything," she said.

During the day, Tonga agreed with her. At night, he still snuggled close to her side. He was still not convinced.

One night, Tonga heard a terrible sound and was afraid. He started to cry.

"Listen, Tonga. That is your father. He is roaring. He is the ruler of the jungle. "Now look at your claws, Son. You can pull them back in, but they are very sharp. Feel your teeth. They are strong and sharp. You are a lion. You are growing bigger. Soon you will go on a hunt," Tonga's mother said.

The next night, Tonga's mother told him to go out a little way into the jungle by himself. Tonga stayed out for a while and then came home. Each night, Tonga spent more time alone in the jungle. He listened to his father's roar and wasn't afraid. He heard other sounds and wasn't afraid.

One morning, some wild dogs came near Tonga and his mother. Without thinking, he ran up to them and let out a roar. It wasn't a very loud roar yet, but the wild dogs ran away. He stood as tall as he could and thought to himself, "I am not afraid. I have protected my mother. I am strong and brave. I am a lion." He let out another roar.

 GO

21

Say It's time to stop. You have finished Lesson 3b.

Review the answers with the students. If any questions caused particular difficulty, work through the stories, questions, and answer choices. Have volunteers explain what these questions are asking.

Have the students indicate completion of the lesson by entering their score for this activity on the progress chart at the beginning of the book. Provide the students whatever help is necessary to record their scores.

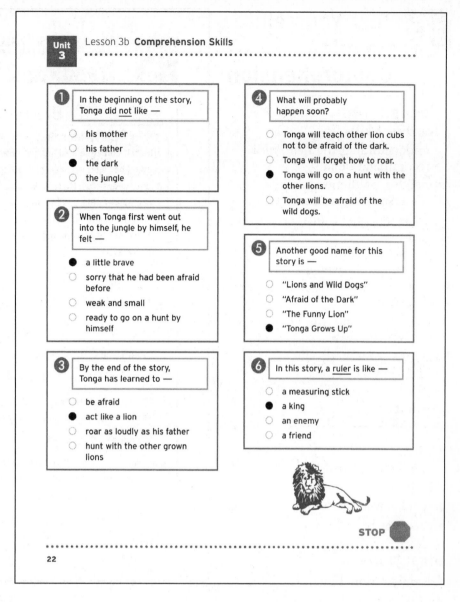

Unit 3 Test Yourself: Reading Comprehension

Focus

Reading Skills
- understanding the main idea
- recognizing details
- making predictions
- understanding reasons
- drawing conclusions

Test-taking Skills
- skimming a passage
- referring to a passage to answer questions
- identifying and using key words to find the answer
- working methodically
- rereading questions
- reasoning from facts and evidence

This lesson simulates an actual test-taking experience. Therefore, it is recommended that the directions be read verbatim and the suggested procedures be followed.

Directions

Administration Time:
approximately 40 minutes

Say Turn to the Test Yourself lesson on page 23.

Check to be sure the students have found the right page. Point out to the students that this Test Yourself lesson is like a real test, but that they will score it themselves to see how well they are doing. Explain that it is important to answer as many questions as possible. Remind the students to listen carefully and to take the best guess when they are unsure of the answer.

Say This lesson will check how well you remember the comprehension skills you practiced in other lessons. Be sure your answer spaces are completely filled in. Press your pencil firmly so that your marks come out dark. Completely erase any marks for answers that you change. Do not write anything except your answers in your book.

Unit 3 Test Yourself: Reading Comprehension

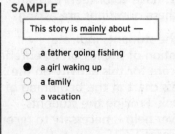

Early Morning

Rita felt someone shaking her. She blinked her eyes and saw her father standing over her. Half-awake, she remembered this was the day they would go fishing in the river. She jumped out of bed and got ready quickly.

SAMPLE

This story is <u>mainly</u> about —

○ a father going fishing
● a girl waking up
○ a family
○ a vacation

Sisters Sharing

"It is my piece of cake!" said Jane.

"I want some of it," said her sister Sue. "You must share with me."

"No, no, no, it is mine. I don't want to share with you," said Jane.

"Girls, stop fussing now," said their mother. "Jane, you must share. Sue shared with you yesterday. Don't you remember?"

Jane nodded. Sue smiled.

Mother said, "One of you will cut the piece of cake in two. The other one will have the first choice of pieces."

GO

23

Find the Sample at the top of the page. Read the story to yourself. *(pause)* Now read the question to yourself while I read it aloud. *This story is <u>mainly</u> about—a father going fishing ... a girl waking up ... a family ... a vacation.* Mark the space for your answer.

Allow time for the students to mark their answers.

Say You should have filled in the second answer space because the story is mainly about *a girl waking up.* If you did not fill in the second space, erase your answer and fill in the second answer space now.

Check to see that the students have marked the correct space.

Say Now you will do some items by yourself. Skim the stories then read the questions and answer them in the same way that we did the Sample. Look back at the stories to answer the questions. If you are not sure which answer is correct, take your best guess. When you see a GO sign at the bottom of a page, go on to the next page and continue working. Work until you come to the STOP sign at the bottom of page 27. Completely erase any marks for answers that you change. Do you have any questions? Start working now.

Allow time for the students to fill in their answers. Walk around the room and provide test-taking tips as necessary.

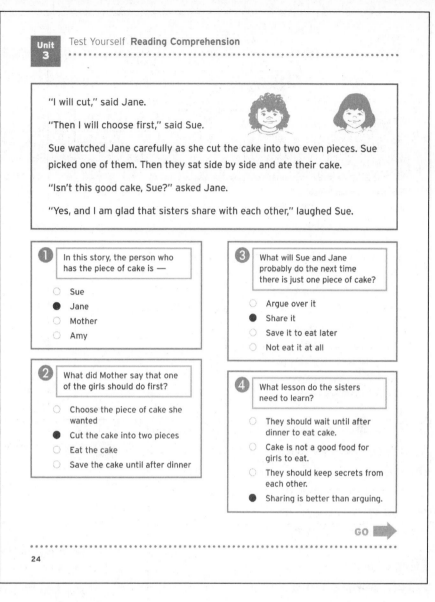

Unit 3 Test Yourself **Reading Comprehension**

"I will cut," said Jane.

"Then I will choose first," said Sue.

Sue watched Jane carefully as she cut the cake into two even pieces. Sue picked one of them. Then they sat side by side and ate their cake.

"Isn't this good cake, Sue?" asked Jane.

"Yes, and I am glad that sisters share with each other," laughed Sue.

1 In this story, the person who has the piece of cake is —
- ○ Sue
- ● Jane
- ○ Mother
- ○ Amy

2 What did Mother say that one of the girls should do first?
- ○ Choose the piece of cake she wanted
- ● Cut the cake into two pieces
- ○ Eat the cake
- ○ Save the cake until after dinner

3 What will Sue and Jane probably do the next time there is just one piece of cake?
- ○ Argue over it
- ● Share it
- ○ Save it to eat later
- ○ Not eat it at all

4 What lesson do the sisters need to learn?
- ○ They should wait until after dinner to eat cake.
- ○ Cake is not a good food for girls to eat.
- ○ They should keep secrets from each other.
- ● Sharing is better than arguing.

GO ➡

24

Birdhouse

Making a birdhouse is fun and easy. Remember, though, you will need some help with cutting.

Use a large, empty, plastic bleach bottle or other large plastic bottle. Wash it out well. Punch two holes just below the lid. Tie a string through these holes. Leave a loop to hang the birdhouse.

Cut a hole near the bottom for the birds to enter. The hole should be about 2 inches wide. Different kinds of birds like holes of different sizes.

Glue a foil pie pan to the bottom of the bleach bottle. The birds can stand on this. Putting some seeds in the pan will attract birds to the house. When they see the opening, they will want to build a nest in it.

Hang your birdhouse in a nearby tree. Hang it high enough so cats will not be able to get to it.

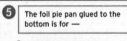 **5** The foil pie pan glued to the bottom is for —

- ● the birds to stand on
- ○ hanging the birdhouse in the tree
- ○ keeping cats out of the birdhouse
- ○ the bird to build a nest

 6 What will make the birdhouse best for a small bird?

- ○ Washing it out
- ● A small hole
- ○ Lots of seed
- ○ A large hole

An Unusual Job

Mr. Johnson is a pet store owner. He has a job many people would like. He gets to take care of and play with lots of animals. He talks to people about what kind of pets they would like to have. He helps them learn to take care of their pets.

Not all pet store jobs are fun. Someone must clean the animals' cages. Their food must be put out every day. The water must be changed. Some of the pets must also be taken out for walks or allowed to <u>exercise</u>.

The pet store owner must have good reading and math skills. Mr. Johnson must read about new foods for the animals. He must know how to use numbers well when he runs his business.

The best part of his job is seeing a boy or girl get just the right pet. Mr. Johnson likes knowing that the child and the animal will soon be best friends.

 7 The part of his job that Mr. Johnson likes best is —

- ○ reading about new foods for the animals
- ● helping each child get the right pet
- ○ cleaning the animals' cages
- ○ doing the math to run his business

8 In this story, <u>exercise</u> is —

- ○ playing games like basketball
- ● letting animals walk or run around
- ○ what Mr. Johnson likes to do after work
- ○ letting the pets rest

GO

Say It's time to stop. You have completed the Test Yourself lesson.

Review the answers with the students. Have the students indicate completion of the lesson by entering their score for this activity on the progress chart at the beginning of the book. Provide the students whatever help is necessary to record their scores.

Rainbows and Clouds

This is a special dessert that your family will enjoy. You will need three packages of colored gelatin mix, water, whipped topping, measuring cup, spoon, and a large plate.

Mix one package of gelatin. Heat one cup of water in the microwave for a minute. Stir in the gelatin powder. Mix well. Add one cup of cold water. Stir again. Pour this into the pan or dish. It will be a thin layer. Put it in the refrigerator for an hour or until it has set.

Mix the second package of gelatin the same way. Carefully pour it over the first layer in the dish. Let it chill for an hour or until it is set.

Mix the third package. Pour it over the other layers. Chill for an hour.

Cut the rainbow gelatin into squares. Carefully lift each square out of the dish. Set them on a plate. Add a "cloud" of whipped topping on one corner. This recipe makes several servings.

---

 9 After you mix the hot water, cold water, and gelatin powder, you should —

- ○ add more cold water
- ○ add the whipped topping
- ● pour it into the pan or dish
- ○ cut it into squares

 10 A good time to make this dessert is —

- ○ in the morning before school
- ● on a rainy Saturday afternoon
- ○ at night before going to bed
- ○ just before you leave on a trip

STOP

27

Background

This unit contains three lessons that deal with mathematics problem-solving skills. Students answer a variety of questions covering a broad range of mathematics skills.

• In Lessons 4a and 4b, students solve a variety of mathematics items involving concepts, problem solving, geometry, and measurement. Students practice listening carefully, finding the answer without computing, and identifying and using key words, figures, and numbers to find the answer. They refer to a graphic, use charts and graphs, and mark the right answer as soon as it is found. Students also work methodically and take the best guess when unsure of the answer.

• In the Test Yourself lesson, the mathematics problem-solving and test-taking skills introduced and used in Lessons 4a and 4b are reinforced and presented in a format that gives students the experience of taking an achievement test.

Instructional Objectives

Lesson 4a **Problem Solving** Lesson 4b **Problem Solving**	Given an oral mathematics problem, students identify which of four answer choices is correct.
Test Yourself	Given questions similar to those in Lessons 4a and 4b, students utilize mathematics problem-solving skills and test-taking strategies on achievement-test formats.

Unit 4 Lesson 4a
Problem Solving

Focus
Mathematics Skills
- understanding place value
- counting
- recognizing numbers
- recognizing fractional parts
- recognizing ordinal numbers
- understanding number sentences
- comparing and ordering numbers
- interpreting tables and graphs
- understanding mathematics language
- recognizing basic shapes
- understanding a calendar
- solving oral word problems

Test-taking Skills
- listening carefully
- finding the answer without computing
- identifying and using key words, figures, and numbers to find the answer
- referring to a graphic
- using charts and graphs
- marking the right answer as soon as it is found

SAMPLE

428	100	8	4	2
	○	○	●	○

Listen carefully while you look at the item.

1

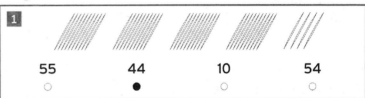

55	44	10	54
○	●	○	○

2

362	326	30062	36200
●	○	○	○

3

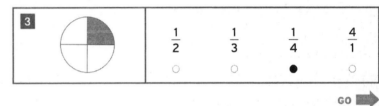

	$\frac{1}{2}$	$\frac{1}{3}$	$\frac{1}{4}$	$\frac{4}{1}$
	○	○	●	○

GO ➡

28

Sample

Distribute scratch paper to the students.

Say Turn to Lesson 4a on page 28. The page number is at the bottom of the page on the left.

Check to see that the students have found the right page.

Say In this lesson, you will work on mathematics problems. When you answer a question, mark the space for the answer you think is right. Be sure your answer space is completely filled in with a dark mark and that you have marked the correct space for the answer you think is right. Find the Sample at the top of the page.

Check to see that the students have found the Sample.

Say Look at the number at the beginning of the row and the answer choices. Which numeral is in the hundreds place in the number? *(pause)* The numeral 4 is in the hundreds place. Mark the space under the numeral *4*. Make sure the space is completely filled in with a dark mark.

Check to see that the students have filled in the correct answer space. If necessary, review the concept of place value, including ones, tens, hundreds, and thousands.

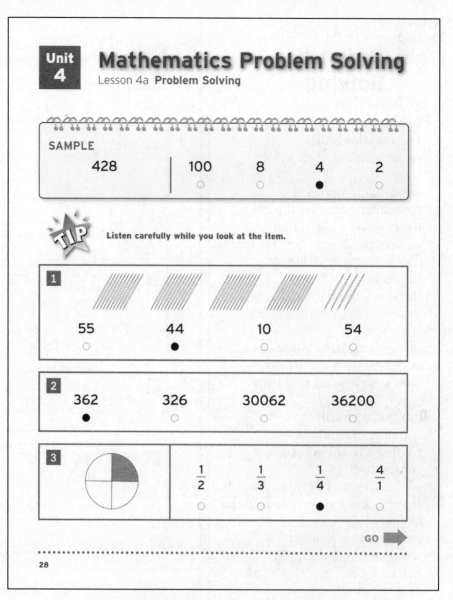

Say Now let's look at the tip.

Read the tip aloud to the students.

Say It is very important for you to listen carefully when I read the items. Look at the item and think about what I am saying. As soon as you know which answer is correct, mark the circle. Don't try to go back and answer questions after we have finished. You will probably have forgotten the question and will probably choose the wrong answer.

Practice

Say Now you are going to do more problems in the same way that we did the Sample. Listen carefully to the question while you look at the item. Do not write anything except your answer choices in your book. If you think it will help, you may do your work on the scratch paper I gave you. As soon as you think you know which answer is correct, fill in the space and listen for the next item. Make sure that the spaces for your answer choices are completely filled in with dark marks. Completely erase any marks for answers that you change. Do you have any questions? Let's begin.

Answer any questions the students have. Allow time between items for students to fill in their answers.

Say Move down to the first row. Donte is using toothpicks for a math project. He counted out this many toothpicks. How many toothpicks did he count?

2. Go to Number 2. Mark under three hundred sixty-two.

3. Look at the last row. What fraction of this shape is shaded?

Check to be sure the students have filled in their answer spaces correctly.

Say Look at the next page, page 29.

Check to be sure the students are on the right page.

Say Find Number 4 at the top of the page. Some children were crossing a bridge with a flag at one end. Mark under the child who is fifth from the flag.

5. Go down to Number 5. Mark under the numeral for two hundred plus twenty.

6. Look at the cars in Number 6. One number sentence that tells about this picture is seven minus three equals four. Which sentence also describes the picture?

7. Move down to the last row. Mark under the number that is between 78 and 112.

Say Look at the next page, page 30.

Check to be sure the students are on the right page.

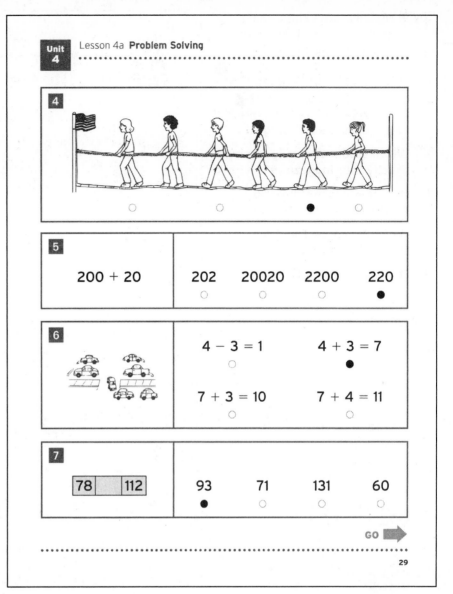

Say In Mr. Rayborn's class, some students counted how many magazines their families received. The graph shows the name of each student and the number of magazines each family received. Use the graph to do Numbers 8 through 10.

8. Which student's family received exactly four magazines?

9. How many magazines did Andy's family receive?

10. Which family received the fewest magazines?

Say Look at the next page, page 31.

Check to be sure the students are on the right page.

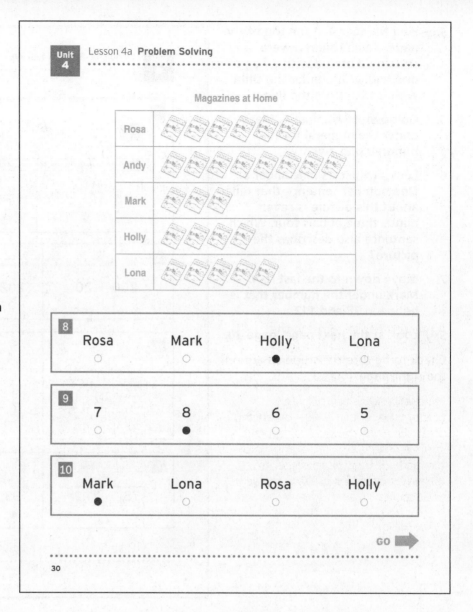

Say Look at the first row at the top of the page, Number 11. Which of these names the least number of things?

12. Go down to Number 12. What number goes in the box to make the sentence true?

13. Move down to the next row. Which is a pair of triangles?

14. Go down to Number 14. Look at the calendar. On what day of the week is September 14? Is it Sunday, Tuesday, Thursday, or Saturday?

    It's time to stop. You have finished Lesson 4a.

Review the answers with the students. If any items caused particular difficulty, work through them with the students.

Have the students indicate completion of the lesson by entering their score for this activity on the progress chart at the beginning of the book. Provide the students whatever help is necessary to record their scores.

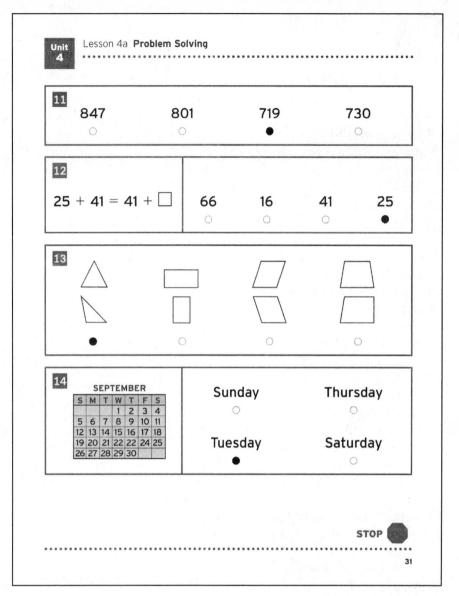

Unit 4

Lesson 4b
Problem Solving

Focus

Mathematics Skills
- understanding place value
- counting
- recognizing numbers
- recognizing fractional parts
- recognizing ordinal numbers
- understanding number sentences
- comparing and ordering numbers
- interpreting tables and graphs
- understanding mathematics language
- recognizing basic shapes
- understanding a calendar
- solving oral word problems

Test-taking Skills
- listening carefully
- finding the answer without computing
- referring to a graphic
- using charts and graphs
- working methodically
- taking the best guess when unsure of the answer

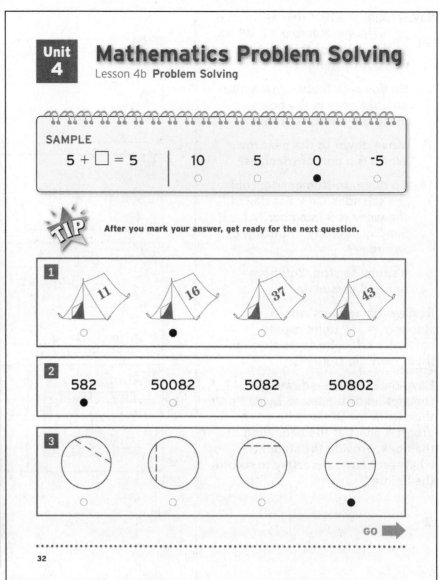

Sample

Distribute scratch paper to the students.

Say Turn to Lesson 4b on page 32. The page number is at the bottom of the page on the left.

Check to see that the students have found the right page.

Say In this lesson, you will solve more mathematics problems. Find the Sample at the top of the page. Look at the problem. What number goes in the box to make this sentence true? *(pause)* The third answer is correct. Mark the space under the third answer. Make sure the space is completely filled in with a dark mark.

Check to see that the students have marked the correct space.

TIP

Say Now let's look at the tip.

Read the tip aloud to the students.

Say It is important that you listen carefully to the problems I read. After you mark an answer, get ready for the next problem. Look at the answer choices and listen to what I say. You should think only about the problem I am reading. If you are not sure which answer is correct, take your best guess.

---

38   **Unit 4**   Lesson 4b **Problem Solving**

Practice

Say You are going to do more problems in the same way that we did the Sample. Listen carefully to the question while you look at the item. Do not write anything except your answer choices in your book. If you think it will help, you may do your work on the scratch paper I gave you. As soon as you think you know which answer is correct, fill in the space and listen for the next item. Make sure that the spaces for your answer choices are completely filled in with dark marks. Completely erase any marks for answers that you change. Do you have any questions? Let's begin.

Answer any questions the students have. Allow time between items for students to fill in their answers.

Say Move down to Number 1. Tasha is at summer camp. She lives in a tent with an even number. In which tent does Tasha live?

2. Go to Number 2. Mark under the number that means five hundreds, eight tens, and two ones.

3. Go to Number 3. Stan drew a circle and divided it in half with a line. Which circle did Stan draw?

Check to be sure the students have filled in their answer spaces correctly.

Say Look at the next page, page 33.

Check to be sure the students are on the right page.

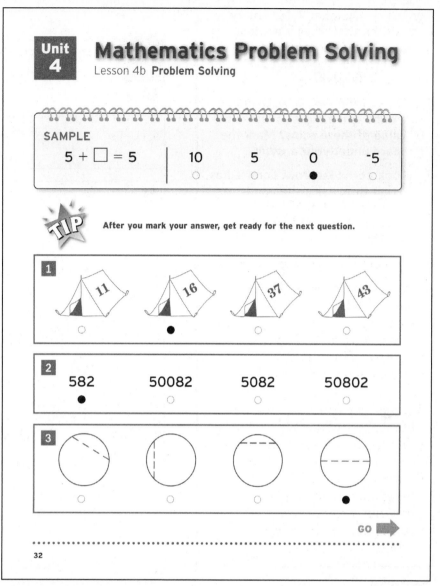

Unit 4 **Mathematics Problem Solving**
Lesson 4b **Problem Solving**

SAMPLE

$5 + \square = 5$ | 10   5   0   -5

TIP After you mark your answer, get ready for the next question.

1. 11   16   37   43

2. 582   50082   5082   50802

3.

GO

32

Say Look at Number 4. Mr. Lowry noticed that there were seven bees in his garden. Mark the circle under the group that shows seven bees.

5. Look at the next row. Gary had a dime and a nickel. What is the value of these coins? Mark the space under your answer.

6. Look at the last row. Loretta has a pair of toy skis she wants to make into a pin. About how long are the skis? Mark your answer.

Say Look at the next page, page 34.

Check to be sure the students are on the right page.

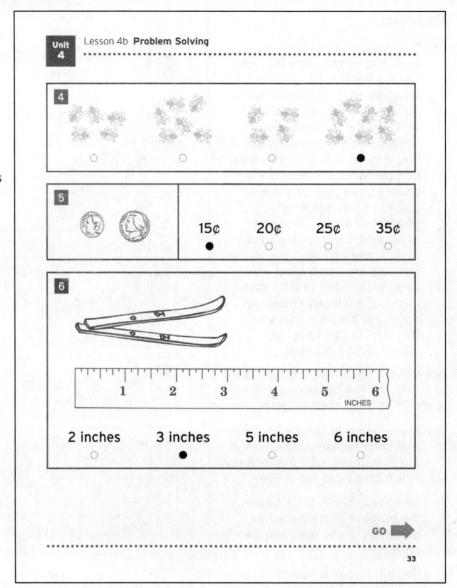

Say Find Number 7 at the top of the page. Here are two dimes. Mark under the amount that is the same as two dimes.

8. Move down to Number 8. Jasmine uses these coins to buy the toy dinosaur. Mark under the money Jasmine has left after buying the toy dinosaur.

9. Move down to the last problem. Terry had eight potatoes to peel. He has already peeled five of them. Which number sentence shows how many potatoes Terry has left to peel?

Say Look at the next page, page 35.

Check to be sure the students are on the right page.

7

2¢   10¢   20¢   50¢
○   ○   ●   ○

8

2¢   10¢   12¢   15¢
○   ○   ●   ○

9

8 − 5 = ☐   5 + 8 = ☐
   ●   ○

8 + 5 = ☐   ☐ − 8 = 5
   ○   ○

GO

34

Say Move your finger under the first row at the top of the next page. This is Number 10. Find a three-digit number less than 500. Each of the number's three digits is an odd number. Mark your answer.

11. Move down to Row 11. Listen to this number puzzle. Find a number that is both inside the triangle and outside the circle. You use this number when you count by fives. Mark under your answer.

12. Move under the last row. Look at the clock. Which answer is the time the clock shows? Mark the space for your answer.

   It's time to stop. You have finished Lesson 4b.

Review the answers with the students. If any items caused particular difficulty, work through them with the students. Encourage volunteers to solve the problems on the board.

Have the students indicate completion of the lesson by entering their score for this activity on the progress chart at the beginning of the book. Provide the students whatever help is necessary to record their scores.

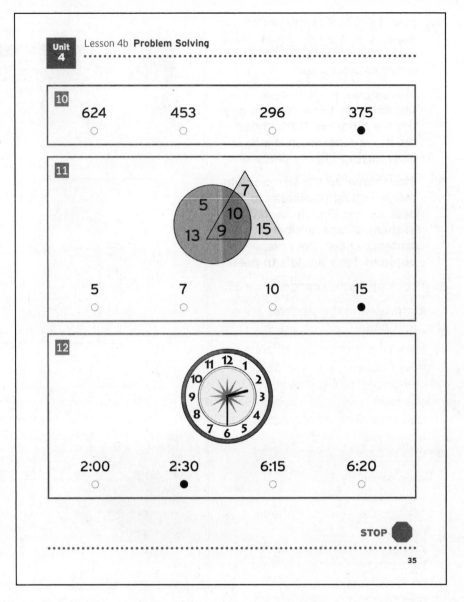

Unit 4
Test Yourself: Mathematics Problem Solving

Focus
Mathematics Skills
- recognizing numbers
- understanding the base-ten system
- recognizing arithmetic fact families
- recognizing fractional parts
- understanding probability
- interpreting tables and graphs
- telling time
- solving number puzzles
- recognizing the value of coins
- understanding number sentences
- comparing and ordering numbers
- understanding mathematics language
- understanding symmetry

Test-taking Skills
- listening carefully
- finding the answer without computing
- identifying and using key words, figures, and numbers to find the answer
- referring to a graphic
- using charts and graphs
- marking the right answer as soon as it is found
- working methodically
- taking the best guess when unsure of the answer

This lesson simulates an actual test-taking experience. Therefore, it is recommended that the directions be read verbatim and the suggested procedures be followed.

Directions
Administration Time: approximately 35 minutes

Distribute scratch paper to the students.

Say Turn to the Test Yourself lesson on page 36.

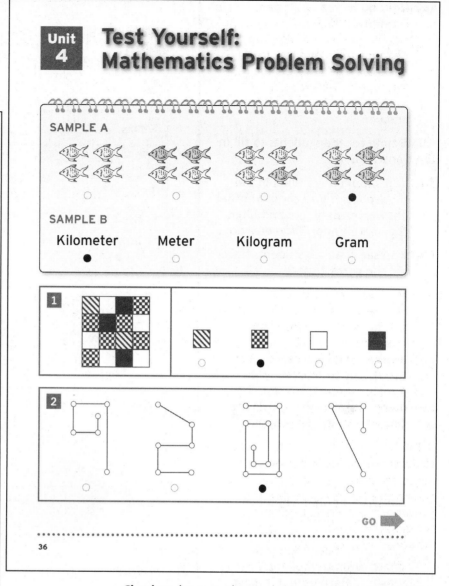

Check to be sure the students have found the right page. Point out to the students that this is not a real test and that they will score it themselves to see how well they are doing.

Say This lesson will check how well you remember the mathematics skills you practiced in other lessons. Put your finger on Sample A at the top of the page. Look at the groups of fish. Mark the space under the group in which three fourths of the fish are shaded.

Allow time for the students to fill in their answers.

Say You should have filled in the last space. If you chose another answer, erase yours and fill in the last space now.

Check to see that the students have marked the correct space.

Say Now do Sample B. Listen carefully. Which metric unit would you use to measure the distance from one city to another? The answers are—*Kilometer* ... *Meter* ... *Kilogram* ... *Gram.* Mark your answer.

Allow time for the students to fill in their answers.

Say You should have filled in the first space. If you chose another answer, erase yours and fill in the space under *Kilometer* now.

Check to see that the students have marked the correct space.

Say Now you will do more mathematics problems. You may use the scratch paper I gave you. When you fill in your answers, make sure you fill in the spaces completely with dark marks. Completely erase any marks for answers you change. Are you ready? Let's begin.

Allow time between items for the students to fill in their answers.

Say Move down to Number 1. Marsha invented a game in which the players drop a beanbag on a board. If a player dropped a beanbag on this board without looking, on which pattern would it most likely fall? Mark your answer.

2. Go to Number 2. For a science project, Juan traced the path made by some insects. Which path is the longest?

   Look at the next page, page 37.

Check to be sure the students are on the right page.

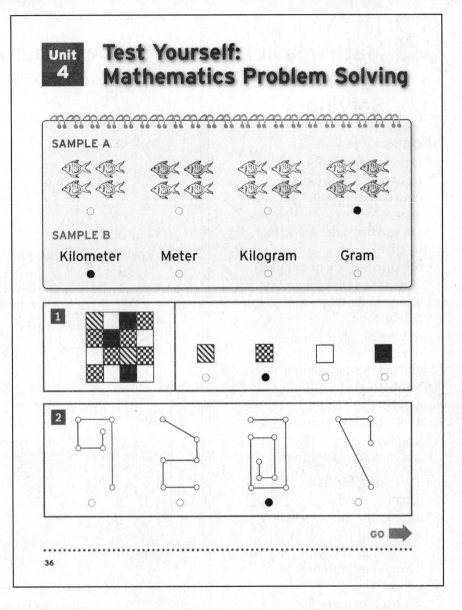

Say Find Number 3 at the top of the page. Listen carefully. I am a number less than 700. Only one of my digits is an odd number. Which number could I be? Mark the space for your answer.

4. Move down to Number 4. What time is shown on the clock?

5. Look at Number 5. At the beginning of the row is a shape with a piece missing. Mark under the shape that is the missing piece.

6. Go down to the last row. Look at the picture of a shark and a shell. About how many shells long is the shark? Mark your answer.

   Look at the next page, page 38.

Check to be sure the students are on the right page.

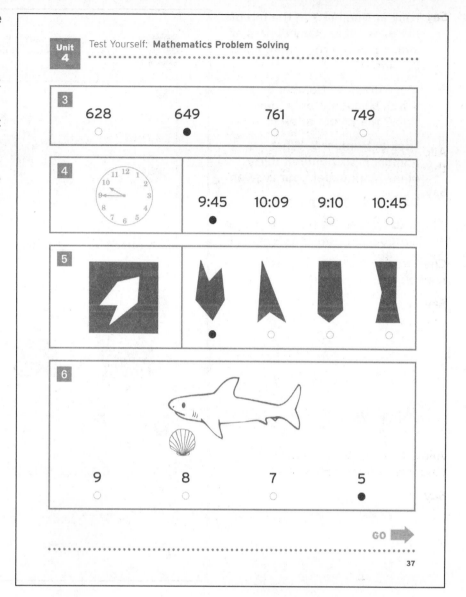

Say Look at Number 7 at the top of
the page. How many ounces of
milk are in the cup? Mark under
the answer.

8.   Move down to Number 8.
     Which shape has only four
     sides? Mark your answer.

9.   Look at Number 9. What
     number is six hundred thirty-
     nine? Mark under your answer.

     Look at the next page, page 39.

Check to be sure the students are on
the right page. Allow the students a
moment to rest.

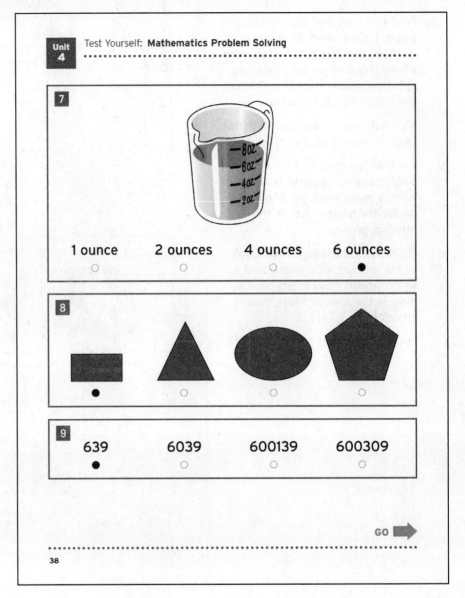

7

1 ounce   2 ounces   4 ounces   6 ounces
   ○   ○   ○   ●

8

   ●   ○   ○   ○

9   639   6039   600139   600309
        ●   ○   ○   ○

GO ➡

38

Say Find Number 10 at the top of the page. There are ten eggs in each basket and some extra eggs. How many eggs are there altogether?

11. Put your finger under Number 11. What numeral is in the ten's place in this number? Mark under your answer.

12. Move down to Number 12. What is two hundred plus seventy? Mark under the answer that shows two hundred plus seventy.

13. Look at Number 13. Mark under the number that means eight hundreds, four tens, and two ones.

14. Look at the answers for Number 14. Which is the least number? Mark under your answer.

Look at the next page, page 40.

Check to be sure the students are on the right page.

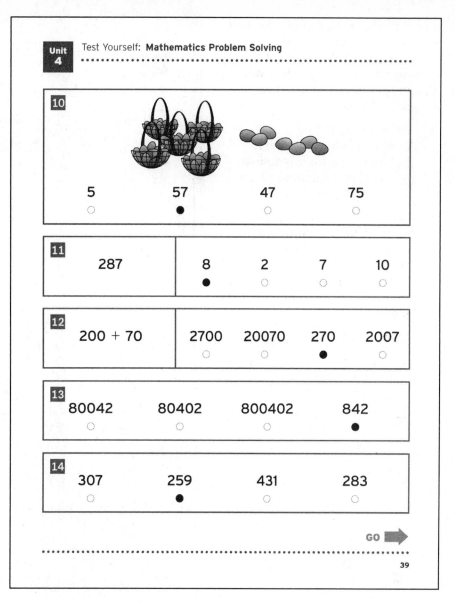

10

5	57	47	75
○	●	○	○

11

287	8	2	7	10
	●	○	○	○

12

200 + 70	2700	20070	270	2007
	○	○	●	○

13

80042	80402	800402	842
○	○	○	●

14

307	259	431	283
○	●	○	○

GO ➡

Say Put your finger under the first row on the page. This is Number 15. Mark under the number that is one hundred more than three hundred seventy-six.

16. Now put your finger under the next row. What number is between one hundred ninety-one and two hundred twenty-four? Mark your answer.

17. Move your finger under Row 17. Seven minus two equals five is a number sentence that describes the balls in this picture. Mark under the sentence that also describes the picture.

Look at the next page, page 41.

Check to be sure the students are on the right page. Allow the students a moment to rest.

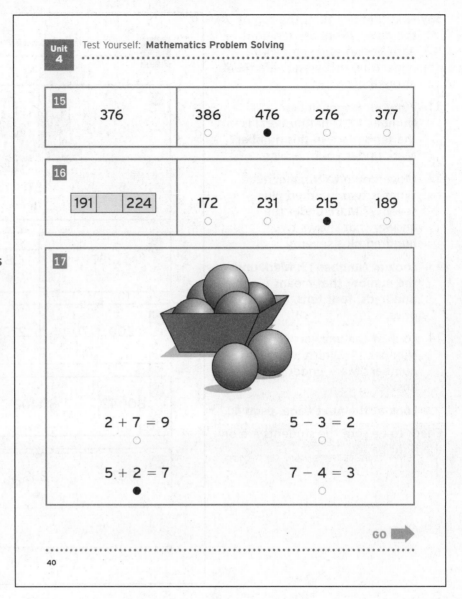

15 376   386 ○   476 ●   276 ○   377 ○

16 | 191 | | 224 | 172 ○   231 ○   215 ●   189 ○

17

$2 + 7 = 9$ ○ $5 - 3 = 2$ ○

$5 + 2 = 7$ ● $7 - 4 = 3$ ○

GO ➡

40

Say Look at Number 18 at the top of the page. What is another way to show two times nine? Mark under the answer.

19. Move down to Number 19. What number goes in the box to make the number sentence true? Mark under your answer.

20. Look at Number 20. What number belongs in the box? Mark your answer. Mark under your answer.

21. Look at the rectangles that have been divided into parts. Mark under the rectangle that has not been divided in half.

It's time to stop. You have completed the Test Yourself lesson.

Review the answers with the students. Have the students indicate completion of the lesson by entering their score for this activity on the progress chart at the beginning of the book. Provide the students whatever help is necessary to record their scores.

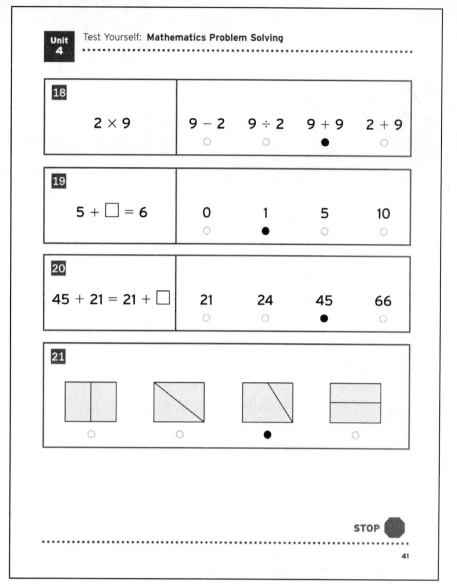

Background

This unit contains three lessons that deal with mathematics procedures. Students answer a variety of oral word problems and computation problems.

• **In Lessons 5a and 5b,** students solve a variety of oral word problems and computation problems. Students learn the importance of analyzing a problem, performing the correct operation, and computing carefully. They transfer numbers accurately, convert items to a workable format, indicate that the correct answer is not given, work methodically, and stay with the first answer.

• **In the Test Yourself lesson,** the mathematics procedures and test-taking skills introduced and used in Lessons 5a and 5b are reinforced and presented in a format that gives students the experience of taking an achievement test.

Instructional Objectives

Lesson 5a **Procedures** Lesson 5b **Procedures**	Given an oral word problem, students identify which of four answer choices is correct or indicate that the correct answer is not given. Given a computation problem, students identify which of four answer choices is correct or indicate that the correct answer is not given.
Test Yourself	Given questions similar to those in Lessons 5a and 5b, students utilize mathematics procedures and test-taking strategies on achievement-test formats.

Focus

Mathematics Skills
- solving oral word problems
- adding whole numbers

Test-taking Skills
- analyzing a problem
- performing the correct operation
- computing carefully
- transferring numbers accurately
- converting items to a workable format
- indicating that the correct answer is not given

Samples A and B

Distribute scratch paper to the students.

Say Turn to Lesson 5a on page 42. The page number is at the bottom of the page on the left.

Check to see that the students have found the right page.

Say In this lesson, you will solve different mathematics problems. Look at Sample A in the box at the top of the page. You will see a picture of some rocks. Listen carefully now. *Five rocks were in a pile. Kamiesha carried two of them to the garden. How may rocks were left on the pile?* Now look at the answer choices. You see the numbers *ten, seven, three, two,* and the letters *NH,* which mean *Not here.* Which answer is correct? Five rocks were in a pile. Kamiesha carried two of them to the garden. How may rocks were left on the pile? *(pause)* The correct answer is *3.* Fill in the space under *3* for Sample A. Make sure the space is completely filled in with a dark mark.

Check to see that the students have marked the correct space.

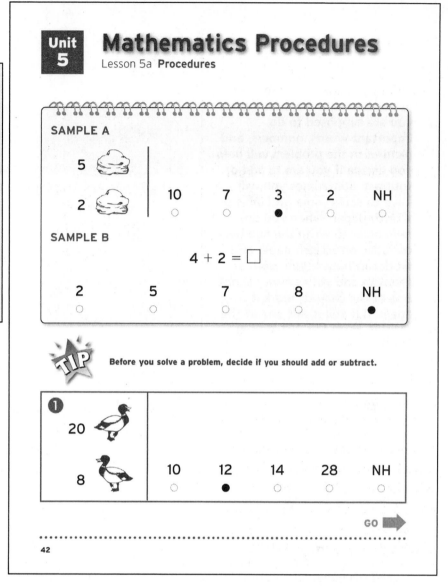

Unit 5
Mathematics Procedures
Lesson 5a **Procedures**

Say Now do Sample B. What is four plus two? *(pause)* Is the answer *two, five, seven, eight,* or is the answer *Not here?* Yes, four plus two is six, but six is not one of the answer choices. Fill in the last space for Sample B because the correct answer, six, is *Not here.* Make sure the answer space is completely filled in with a dark mark.

Check to see that the students have marked the correct space. If necessary, review the solution to each of the sample problems.

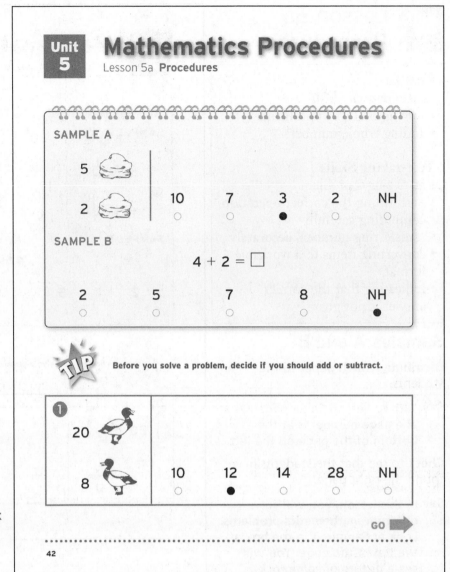

⭐TIP

Say Now let's look at the tip.

Read the tip aloud to the students.

Say Before you solve the problems in this lesson, think about what you are supposed to do. Important words, numbers, and pictures in the problem will help you decide if you are to add or subtract. Sometimes you will have to solve some problems on scratch paper. When you do, remember to write the numbers correctly on scratch paper and work carefully. If you work a problem and your answer is not one of the choices, work it again. If it still is not one of the choices, mark the last answer, *NH,* for *Not here.*

Practice

Say Now you will do more items. Do not write anything except your answer choices in your book. Remember to listen carefully and think about what you are supposed to do. If you think it will help, you may do your work on the scratch paper I gave you. For some problems, you will have to rearrange the problem on scratch paper so you can solve it. When you have finished working a problem, fill in the space for your answer. Remember to mark the last answer choice, *NH,* if the correct answer is not one of the choices. Make sure that the spaces for your answer choices are completely filled in with dark marks. Completely erase any marks for answers that you change. Let's begin.

Allow time between items for students to fill in their answers.

Say Find the first item, the one with the ducks. Listen carefully. Pauline saw twenty ducks on a pond. Eight of the ducks flew away. How many ducks were left on the pond? Mark the space under your answer.

Check to be sure the students have filled in their answer spaces correctly.

Say Look at the next page, page 43.

Check to be sure the students are on the right page.

Say Look at Number 2 at the top of the page. The school cafeteria staff put out thirteen peaches and thirty-three oranges. How many pieces of fruit in all did they put out?

3. Move down to Number 3. A fisherman dug up fifty-six large clams and twenty-nine small clams. How many more large clams did he find than small clams?

4. Look at Number 4. The Powell School pep club ordered seventeen gray pennants and fourteen white pennants. How many pennants did they order in all?

5. Do Number 5 yourself. It is just like Sample B that we did before. Look at the problem and find the answer. You can work on scratch paper if you would like. If the answer you find is not one of the choices, mark the last space, *NH*. Do you have any questions? Start working now.

Allow time for students to fill in their answers.

Say It's time to stop. You have finished Lesson 5a.

Review the answers with the students. If any items caused particular difficulty, work through them with the students.

Have the students indicate completion of the lesson by entering their score for this activity on the progress chart at the beginning of the book. Provide the students whatever help is necessary to record their scores.

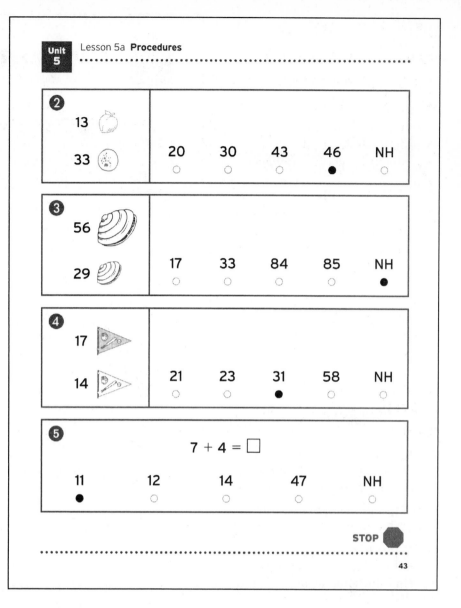

Unit 5 | Lesson 5b
Procedures

Focus

Mathematics Skills
- solving oral word problems
- adding whole numbers
- subtracting whole numbers

Test-taking Skills
- performing the correct operation
- computing carefully
- transferring numbers accurately
- converting items to a workable format
- indicating that the correct answer is not given
- working methodically
- staying with the first answer

Samples A and B

Distribute scratch paper to the students.

Say Turn to Lesson 5b on page 44. The page number is at the bottom of the page on the left.

Check to see that the students have found the right page.

Say In this lesson, you will solve more mathematics problems. Find the samples at the top of the page. Look at Sample A and listen to what I say. *A mother seal weighs 319 pounds and a young seal weighs 70 pounds. How much do the seals weigh altogether?* *(pause)* The answer to the problem is *389*. Fill in the space under *389* for Sample A. Make sure the space is completely filled in with a dark mark.

Check to see that the students have marked the correct space.

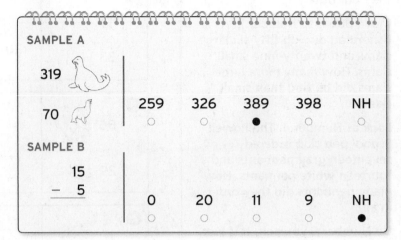

Unit 5 **Mathematics Procedures**
Lesson 5b Procedures

SAMPLE A

319
70

| 259 | 326 | 389 | 398 | NH |
| ○ | ○ | ● | ○ | ○ |

SAMPLE B

15
− 5

| 0 | 20 | 11 | 9 | NH |
| ○ | ○ | ○ | ○ | ● |

TIP Stay with your first answer. Change it only if you are sure it is wrong.

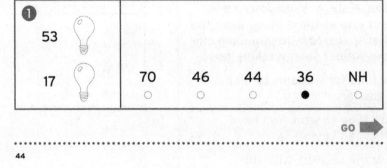

① 53
17

| 70 | 46 | 44 | 36 | NH |
| ○ | ○ | ○ | ● | ○ |

GO →

44

Say Now do Sample B. What is fifteen take away five? *(pause)* Is the answer *zero, twenty, eleven, nine,* or is the answer *Not here*? The solution to the problem is ten, but ten is not one of the answer choices. Fill in the last space for Sample B because the correct answer, ten, is *Not here*. Make sure the answer space is completely filled in with a dark mark.

Check to see that the students have marked the correct space. If necessary, review the solution to each of the sample problems.

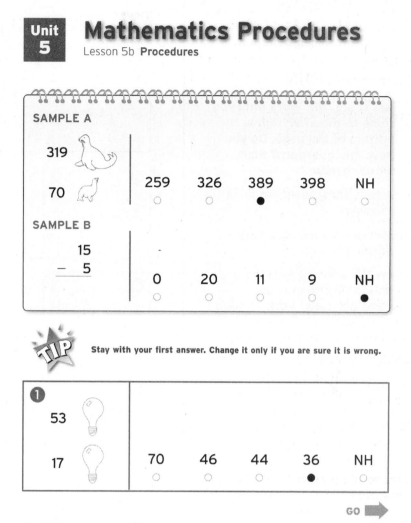

TIP

Say Now let's look at the tip.

Read the tip aloud to the students.

Say Sometimes you may mark an answer and then change your mind. You should do this only if you are sure your first answer in wrong and another answer is better. This is especially important for problems in which I give you directions. You might not remember enough of the problem to find the right answer if you change yours. So remember, change your answer only if you are sure you have made a mistake.

Take a few minutes to discuss with the students the importance of staying with the first answer. Some students lack the confidence to stay with their first answer, yet this is a winning strategy. Explain that they should change their answer only if they are sure their first answer is wrong and another answer is better.

Practice

Say Now you will do more items. Do not write anything except your answer choices in your book. Remember to listen carefully and think about what you are supposed to do. If you work on scratch paper, be sure to copy the numbers correctly and perform the right operation. For some problems, you will have to rearrange the problem on scratch paper so you can solve it. When you have finished working a problem, fill in the space for your answer. Remember to mark the last answer choice, *NH*, if the correct answer is not one of the choices. Make sure that the spaces for your answer choices are completely filled in with dark marks. Completely erase any marks for answers that you change. Let's begin.

Allow time between items for students to fill in their answers.

Say Put your finger under the first problem. In a school gymnasium there are 53 lights. During the year, 17 of the bulbs had to be replaced because they burned out. How many lights did not burn out? Mark your answer.

Say Look at the next page, page 45.

Check to be sure the students are on the right page.

Say You will do the problems on this page by yourself. Look at the problem and find the answer. You can work on scratch paper if you would like. If the answer you find is not one of the choices, mark the last space, *NH.* Work until you come to the STOP sign at the bottom of the page. Do you have any questions? Start working now.

Allow time for students to fill in their answers.

Say It's time to stop. You have finished Lesson 5b.

Review the answers with the students. If any items caused particular difficulty, work through them with the students. Be sure to emphasize each step of the solution to each problem.

Have the students indicate completion of the lesson by entering their score for this activity on the progress chart at the beginning of the book. Provide the students whatever help is necessary to record their scores.

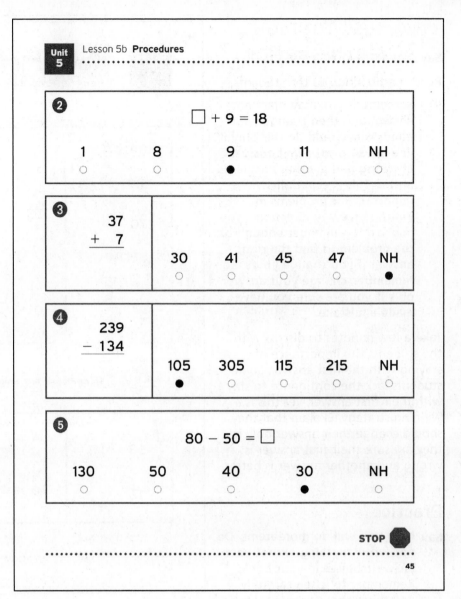

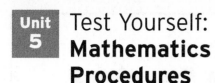

Test Yourself: Mathematics Procedures

Focus

Mathematics Skills
- solving oral word problems
- adding whole numbers
- subtracting whole numbers

Test-taking Skills
- analyzing a problem
- performing the correct operation
- computing carefully
- transferring numbers accurately
- converting items to a workable format
- indicating that the correct answer is not given
- working methodically
- staying with the first answer

This lesson simulates an actual test-taking experience. Therefore, it is recommended that the directions be read verbatim and the suggested procedures be followed.

Directions

Administration Time: approximately 25 minutes

Distribute scratch paper to the students.

Say Turn to the Test Yourself lesson on page 46.

Check to be sure the students have found the right page. Point out to the students that this is not a real test and that they will score it themselves to see how well they are doing.

Say This lesson will check how well you remember the mathematics skills you practiced in other lessons. Find Sample A at the top of the page. At a school picnic, Ms. Leonard's students ate twenty-three sandwiches and seventeen apples. How many sandwiches and apples did they eat altogether? Mark the space for your answer.

Allow time for the students to fill in their answers.

Say You should have filled in the space under the first answer. If you chose another answer, erase yours and fill in the first space now.

Check to see that the students have marked the correct space.

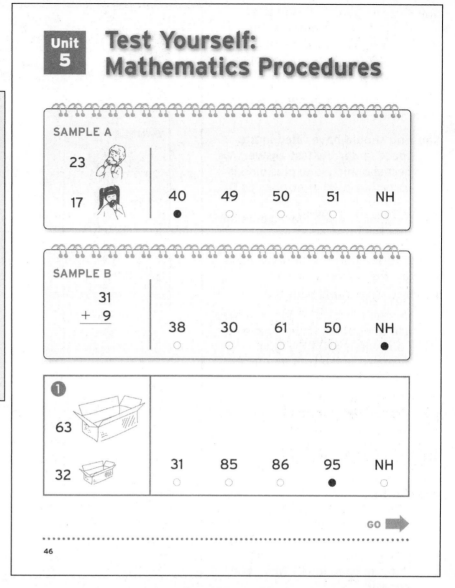

Say Now do Sample B. What is thirty-one plus nine? Is the answer *38, 30, 61, 50,* or is the answer *Not here?* Mark the space for your answer.

Allow time for the students to fill in their answers.

Say You should have filled in the space under the last answer, *NH,* because thirty-one plus nine is forty, but forty is not one of the answer choices. If you chose another answer, erase yours and fill in the last space now.

Check to see that the students have marked the correct space.

Say Now you will do more mathematics problems. You may use the scratch paper I gave you. When you fill in your answers, make sure you fill in the spaces completely with dark marks. Completely erase any marks for answers you change. Let's begin.

Allow time between items for the students to fill in their answers.

Say Put your finger under the first problem. At a shipping company, the clerk has sixty-three large boxes and thirty-two small boxes. How many boxes does he have in all? Mark your answer.

Look at the next page, page 47.

Check to be sure the students are on the right page. Allow the students a moment to rest.

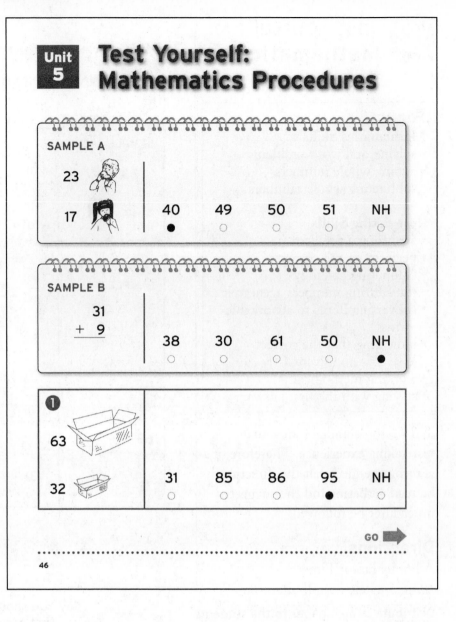

Say Look at Number 2 at the top of the page. Coach Martin bought 60 baseballs at the beginning of the season. The team used 41 baseballs during the season. How many baseballs were left? Mark the space for your answer.

3. Move down to Number 3. A craft store sold 82 candles at one holiday and 24 candles at the next holiday. How many candles did they sell in all? The store sold 82 candles at one holiday and 24 at the next. Mark the space for your answer.

4. Look at Number 4. A school library has 71 chairs. Students are sitting in 32 chairs. How many chairs are empty? There are 71 chairs in the library and students are sitting in 32 chairs. How many chairs are empty? Mark your answer.

5. Move down to the last item. At a nature park, there are 29 frogs on the shore and 55 frogs in the water. How many more frogs are in the water than on the shore? There are 55 frogs in the water and 29 on the shore. How many more are in the water? Mark your answer.

Look at the next page, page 48.

Check to be sure the students are on the right page. Allow the students a moment to rest.

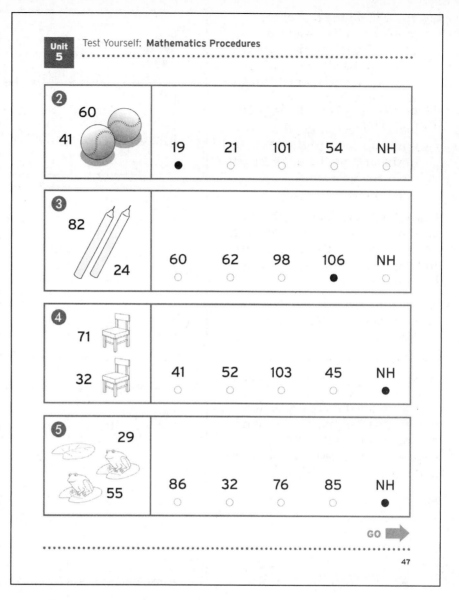

Say You will do the rest of the problems in this lesson by yourself. Look at the problem and find the answer. You can work on scratch paper if you would like. If the answer you find is not one of the choices, mark the last space, *NH.* Work until you come to the STOP sign at the bottom the page. Do you have any questions? Start working now.

Answer any questions the students have. Allow time for the students to complete the items. Encourage the students to use scratch paper when this is appropriate.

Say It's time to stop. You have completed the Test Yourself lesson.

Review the answers with the students. Have the students indicate completion of the lesson by entering their score for this activity on the progress chart at the beginning of the book. Provide the students whatever help is necessary to record their scores.

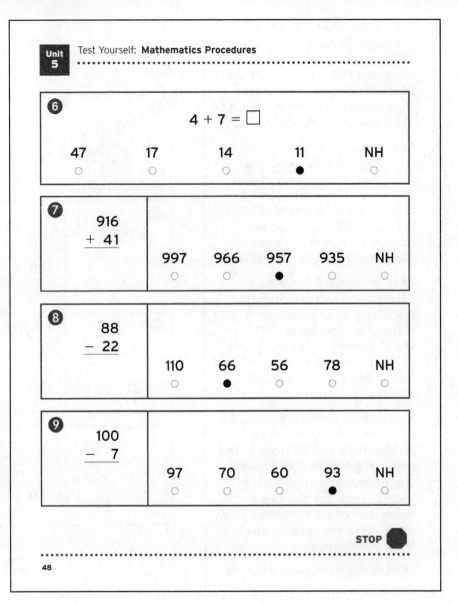

Unit 6

Background

This unit contains three lessons that deal with spelling skills. Students identify the word in a sentence that is spelled incorrectly.

• **In Lessons 6a and 6b,** students find misspelled words in sentences. Students consider every answer choice, compare answer choices, and avoid overanalysis of answer choices. They subvocalize answer choices, search for multiple errors, and work methodically.

• **In the Test Yourself lesson,** the spelling and test-taking skills introduced and used in Lessons 6a and 6b are reinforced and presented in a format that gives students the experience of taking an achievement test.

Instructional Objectives

Lesson 6a **Spelling Skills** Lesson 6b **Spelling Skills**	Given a sentence with underlined words, students identify which of the words is spelled incorrectly.
Test Yourself	Given questions similar to those in Lessons 6a and 6b, students utilize spelling skills and test-taking strategies on achievement-test formats.

Lesson 6a
Spelling Skills

Focus

Spelling Skill
- identifying incorrectly spelled words

Test-taking Skills
- considering every answer choice
- comparing answer choices
- avoiding overanalysis of answer choices
- subvocalizing answer choices

Samples A and B

Say Turn to Lesson 6a on page 49. The page number is at the bottom of the page on the right.

Check to see that the students have found the right page.

Say In this lesson, you will find words that are spelled wrong. Let's do Sample A. Read the sentence to yourself as I read it aloud. *Toss the bal here.* Which underlined word is spelled wrong? *(pause)* The second underlined word is wrong. It should be spelled *b-a-l-l.* Fill in the space under the second underlined word. Check to make sure your answer space is completely filled in with a dark mark.

Check to see that the students have filled in the right answer space.

Say Now we'll do Sample B. Read the sentence to yourself as I read it aloud. *The snow felt very coald.* Which underlined word is spelled wrong? *(pause)* The last underlined word is wrong. It should be spelled *c-o-l-d.* Fill in the space under the last underlined word. Check to make sure your answer space is completely filled in with a dark mark.

Check to see that the students have filled in the right answer space.

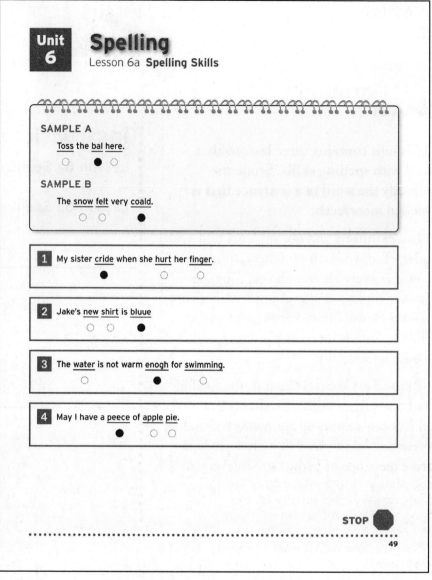

★TIP

Say Now let's look at the tip.

Read the tip aloud to the students.

Say In this lesson, you are supposed to find the word that is misspelled. The first thing you should do is look at each answer choice briefly. Focus on the underlined word, not the other words. But remember, don't spend too much time on an item. If you do, all the words begin to look misspelled. Compare the underlined words with one another until you find the one that looks like it is misspelled. You might also find it helpful to say the underlined word to yourself while you look at it. Saying a word to yourself while you look at it will often help you find the answer that is misspelled.

Practice

Say Now you will do more items yourself. Look for the underlined word that is spelled wrong. Compare the underlined words with one another, and if it helps, say the underlined words to yourself. When you mark your answers, make sure you fill in the spaces with dark marks. Do not write anything except your answer choices in your book. Completely erase any marks for answers that you change. Work until you come to the STOP sign at the bottom of the page. Do you have any questions? Start working now.

Allow time for the students to fill in their answers.

Say It's time to stop. You have finished Lesson 6a.

Review the answers with the students. Have volunteers write the correct spelling of the misspelled words on the board.

Have the students indicate completion of the lesson by entering their score for this activity on the progress chart at the beginning of the book. Provide the students whatever help is necessary to record their scores.

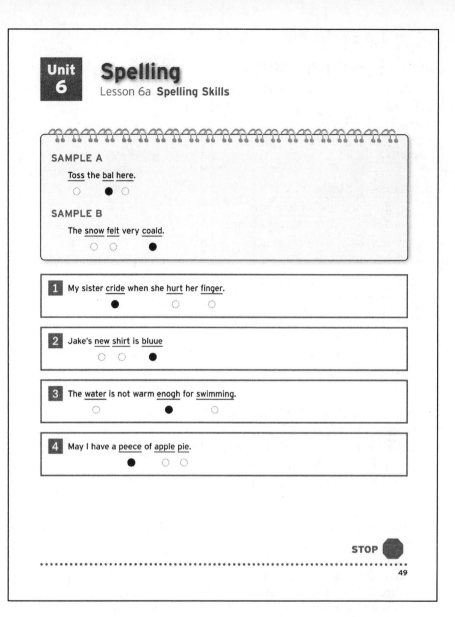

Unit 6 **Spelling**
Lesson 6a **Spelling Skills**

SAMPLE A

Toss the bal here.
○ ● ○

SAMPLE B

The snow felt very coald.
○ ○ ●

1 My sister cride when she hurt her finger.
● ○ ○

2 Jake's new shirt is bluue
○ ○ ●

3 The water is not warm enogh for swimming.
○ ● ○

4 May I have a peece of apple pie.
● ○ ○

STOP

49

Unit 6 Lesson 6b
Spelling Skills

Focus

Spelling Skill
- identifying incorrectly spelled words

Test-taking Skills
- searching for multiple errors
- considering every answer choice
- subvocalizing answer choices
- working methodically

Samples A and B

Say Turn to Lesson 6b on page 50. The page number is at the bottom of the page on the left.

Check to see that the students have found the right page.

Say In this lesson, you will find more words that are spelled wrong. Let's begin by doing Sample A. Read the sentence to yourself as I read it aloud. *The family lived in a big house.* Which of the underlined words is misspelled? *(pause)* The first underlined word is misspelled. The correct spelling is *f-a-m-i-l-y.* Fill in the space under the first underlined word. Check to make sure your answer space is completely filled in with a dark mark.

Check to see that the students have filled in the right answer space.

Say Now do Sample B. Read the sentence for Sample B to yourself. Look carefully at the underlined words. Which of the underlined words is misspelled? *(pause)* The second underlined word is misspelled. The correct spelling is *c-a-k-e.* Fill in the space under the second underlined word. Check to make sure your answer space is completely filled in with a dark mark.

Check to see that the students have filled in the right answer space.

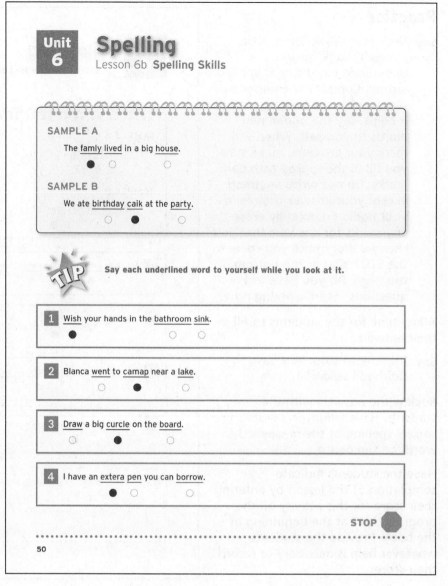

★ TIP

Say Now let's look at the tip.

Have a volunteer read the tip aloud.

Say When you answer spelling items, a good strategy to use is to look carefully at each word as you say it to yourself. This will help you find any words that are misspelled. Think about the different kinds of spelling mistakes. Look for missing letters, extra letters, or letters that are wrong.

Practice

Say Now you will do more items yourself. Look for the underlined word that is spelled wrong. Compare the underlined words with one another, and if it helps, say the underlined words to yourself. When you mark your answers, make sure you fill in the spaces with dark marks. Do not write anything except your answer choices in your book. Completely erase any marks for answers that you change. Work until you come to the STOP sign at the bottom of the page. Do you have any questions? Start working now.

Allow time for the students to fill in their answers.

Say It's time to stop. You have finished Lesson 6b.

Review the answers with the students. Have volunteers read each sentence, identify the misspelled word, and discuss the spelling error.

Have the students indicate completion of the lesson by entering their score for this activity on the progress chart at the beginning of the book. Provide the students whatever help is necessary to record their scores.

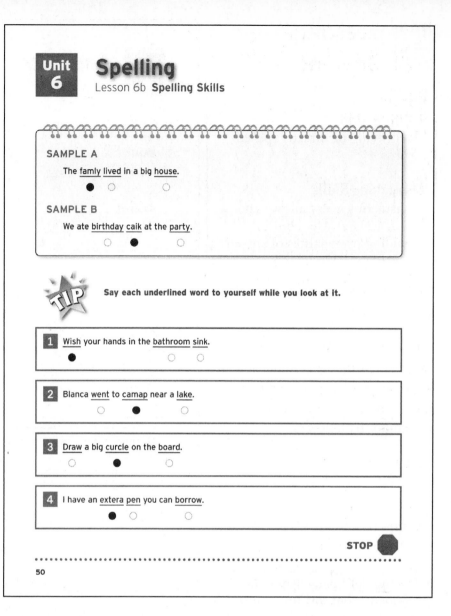

Unit 6

Spelling

Lesson 6b **Spelling Skills**

SAMPLE A

The <u>famly</u> <u>lived</u> in a big <u>house</u>.
● ○ ○

SAMPLE B

We ate <u>birthday</u> <u>caik</u> at the <u>party</u>.
○ ● ○

TIP Say each underlined word to yourself while you look at it.

1 <u>Wish</u> your hands in the <u>bathroom</u> <u>sink</u>.
● ○ ○

2 Blanca <u>went</u> to <u>camap</u> near a <u>lake</u>.
○ ● ○

3 <u>Draw</u> a big <u>curcle</u> on the <u>board</u>.
○ ● ○

4 I have an <u>extera</u> <u>pen</u> you can <u>borrow</u>.
● ○ ○

STOP

50

Focus

Spelling Skill
• identifying incorrectly spelled words

Test-taking Skills
• considering every answer choice
• comparing answer choices
• avoiding overanalysis of answer choices
• subvocalizing answer choices
• searching for multiple errors
• working methodically

This lesson simulates an actual test-taking experience. Therefore, it is recommended that the directions be read verbatim and the suggested procedures be followed.

Directions

Administration Time: approximately 20 minutes

Say Turn to the Test Yourself lesson on page 51.

Check to be sure the students have found the right page. Point out to the students that this Test Yourself lesson is like a real test, but that they will score it themselves to see how well they are doing. Explain that it is important to answer as many questions as possible. Remind the students to listen carefully and to take the best guess when they are unsure of the answer.

Say This lesson will check how well you remember the spelling skills you practiced in other lessons. Be sure your answer spaces are completely filled in. Press your pencil firmly so that your marks come out dark. Completely erase any marks for answers that you change. Do not write anything except your answers in your book. Read the directions at the top of the page to yourself while I read them aloud to you.

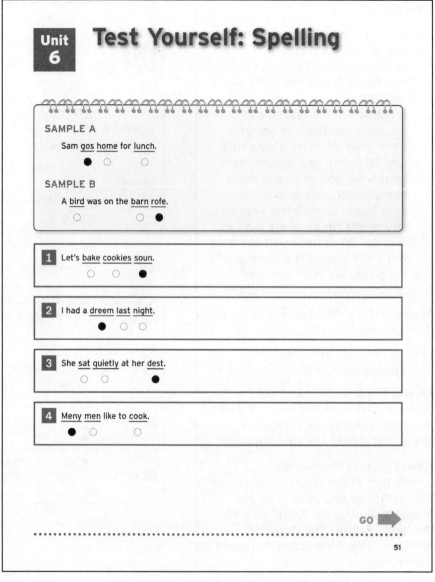

Read the directions aloud.

Say Let's do Sample A. Read the sentence to yourself as I read it aloud. *Sam gos home for lunch.* Which word is misspelled? Mark the space for your answer.

Allow time for the students to fill in their answers.

Say The first underlined word is spelled wrong, so you should have filled in the space under *gos*. The correct spelling of the word is *g-o-e-s*. If you chose another answer, erase yours and fill in the space under the first answer now.

Check to see that the students have marked the correct space.

Say Now do Sample B. Read the sentence to yourself. Which word is misspelled? Mark the space for your answer.

Allow time for the students to fill in their answers.

Say The last word is misspelled, so you should have filled in the last answer space. The correct spelling of the word is *r-o-o-f*. If you chose another answer, erase yours and fill in the space under the last word now.

Check to see that the students have marked the correct space.

Say Now you will do more spelling items yourself. Look for the underlined word that is spelled wrong. When you mark your answers, make sure you fill in the spaces with dark marks. Do not write anything except your answer choices in your book. Completely erase any marks for answers that you change. When you come to the GO sign at the bottom of the page, go on to the next page and continue working. Work until you come to the STOP sign on page 52. Do you have any questions? Start working now.

Allow time for the students to fill in their answers. Walk around the room and provide test-taking tips as necessary.

Say It's time to stop. You have completed the Test Yourself lesson.

Review the answers with the students. Have the students indicate completion of the lesson by entering their score for this activity on the progress chart at the beginning of the book. Provide the students whatever help is necessary to record their scores.

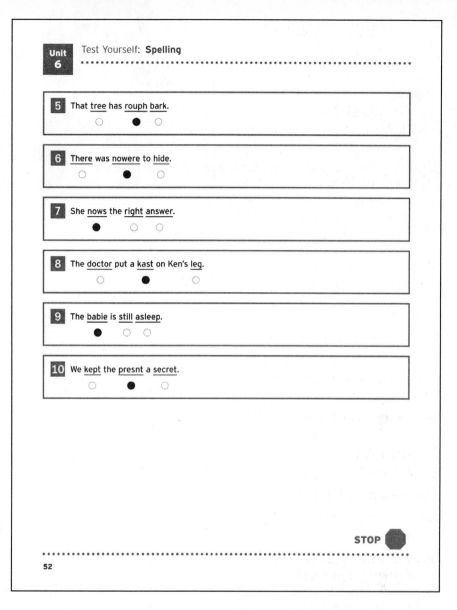

Background

This unit contains three lessons that deal with English language skills. Students answer a variety of questions about grammar, usage, sentence formation, and paragraphs.

• **In Lessons 7a and 7b,** students choose the answer that represents correct capitalization, punctuation, or usage. They answer questions about composition strategies, identify correctly formed sentences, and answer questions about a paragraph. Students show they can listen carefully, mark the right answer as soon as it is found, and indicate that an item has no mistakes. They also compare answer choices, work methodically, stay with the first answer, use context to find the answer, and refer to a passage to answer questions.

• **In the Test Yourself lesson,** the language and test-taking skills introduced and used in Lessons 7a and 7b are reinforced and presented in a format that gives students the experience of taking an achievement test.

Instructional Objectives

Lesson 7a Language Skills **Lesson 7b** Language Skills	Given a sentence with an underlined part, students identify the correct way to write the underlined part or indicate that the part should be written *The way it is.*
	Given a group of words, students identify which of two answer choices is a better way to write the words as a sentence or indicate that it should be written *The way it is.*
	Given a question about composition strategies, students identify which of three answer choices is correct.
	Given a paragraph and questions about it, students identify which of three answer choices is correct.
Test Yourself	Given questions similar to those in Lessons 7a and 7b, students utilize language skills and test-taking strategies on achievement-test formats.

Unit 7
Lesson 7a
Language Skills

Focus

Language Skills
• identifying correct capitalization
• identifying correct punctuation
• choosing correctly used words
• identifying correctly formed sentences
• identifying correct composition strategies
• identifying the best sentence to add to a paragraph
• identifying the main reason for a paragraph

Test-taking Skills
• listening carefully
• marking the right answer as soon as it is found
• indicating that an item has no mistakes
• comparing answer choices
• subvocalizing answer choices

Samples A and B

Say Turn to Lesson 7a on page 53. The page number is at the bottom of the page on the right.

Check to see that the students have found the right page.

Say In this lesson, you will practice your English language skills. When you answer a question, mark the space for the answer you think is right. Be sure your answer space is completely filled in with a dark mark. Find Sample A at the top of the page.

Check to see that the students have found Sample A.

Say Look at Sample A. Read the sentence with the underlined part to yourself while I read it aloud. "Our Aunt is coming for a visit." How should the underlined part be written? Should it be *Aunt are* with a capital A ... *aunt is* with a lower-case a ... or should it be written *The way it is*? (pause) The second answer choice, *aunt is,* is correct. Mark the space beside the second answer for Sample A. Make sure the space is completely filled in with a dark mark.

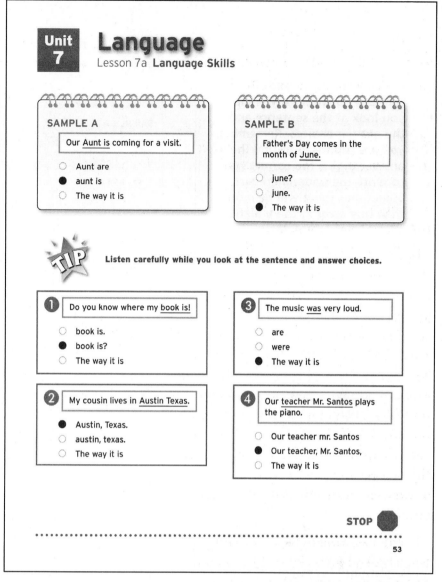

Check to see that the students have marked the correct space. Discuss with the students why the second answer is correct.

Say Now do Sample B. Read the sentence with the underlined part to yourself while I read it aloud. "Father's Day comes in the month of June." How should the underlined part be written? Should it be *june?* with a lower-case j and a question mark ... *june.* with a lower-case j and a period ... or should it be written *The way it is?* (pause) The underlined part is correct, so you should mark the space beside the last answer, *The way it is,* for Sample B. Make sure the space is completely filled in with a dark mark.

Check to see that the students have filled in the correct answer space. Explain why the underlined part of Sample B is correct.

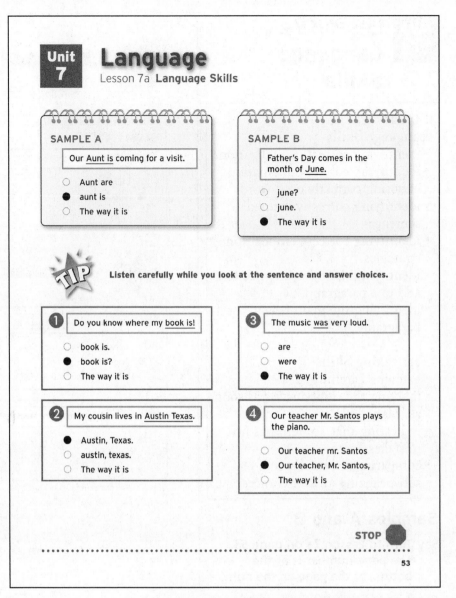

⭐TIP

Say Now let's look at the tip.

Read the tip aloud to the students.

Say In this lesson, you must listen carefully to what I say while you look at the sentence and the answer choices. Remember, you are supposed to find the answer that is the correct way to write the underlined part. Sometimes there will be more than one error in the underlined part, so be careful. If the underlined part is already correct, choose the last answer, *The way it is.*

Practice

Say Now you will do more items. Listen carefully to what I say. If there is an error, find the answer choice that shows the correct way to write the underlined part. If there is no error, choose the last answer choice, *The way it is.* Make sure you fill in the spaces with dark marks. Do not write anything except your answer choices in your book. Completely erase any marks for answers that you change. Do you have any questions? Let's begin.

Answer any questions the students have. Allow time between items for students to fill in their answers.

Say Put your finger under Number 1 below the samples. "Do you know where my <u>book is!</u>" How should the underlined part be written? Look closely at the punctuation and then mark your answer.

2. "My cousin lives in <u>Austin Texas.</u>" How should the underlined part be written? Look closely at the punctuation and capitalization and then mark your answer.

3. "The music <u>was</u> very loud." How should the underlined part be written? Should it be *are …* *were …* or should it be written *The way it is?* Mark your answer.

4. "Our <u>teacher Mr. Santos</u> plays the piano." How should the underlined part be written? Look very closely at the punctuation and capitalization, then mark your answer.

Check to be sure the students have filled in their answer spaces correctly.

Say Look at the next page, page 54.

Check to be sure the students are on the right page.

Samples C and D

Say Now we will do some different items. Look at Sample C in the box at the top of the page. Read the group of words in the box while I read it aloud. "Miguel finding lost treasure in the forest." How should this group of words be written to make a complete and correct sentence? Should it be written *Miguel found lost treasure in the forest. … Miguel finding lost treasure. In the forest. …* or should it be written *The way it is?* (pause) The first answer choice is a complete and correct sentence. Mark the space beside the first answer for Sample C. Make sure the space is completely filled in with a dark mark.

Check to see that the students have filled in the correct space. Discuss with the students why the first answer choice is correct.

Say Move over to Sample D. Read the group of words in the box for Sample D while I read it aloud. "Luke wanted to play baseball with his friends." How should this group of words be written to make a complete and correct sentence? Should it be written *Luke wanted to play baseball. With his friends. … Luke wanting to play baseball with his friends. …* or should it be written *The way it is?* (pause) The last answer choice is correct because the group of words in the box is a complete and correct sentence. Mark the space beside the last answer for Sample D. Make sure the space is completely filled in with a dark mark.

Check to see that the students have filled in the correct answer space.

⭐TIP

Say Now let's look at the tip.

Read the tip aloud to the students.

Unit 7 — Lesson 7a **Language Skills**

SAMPLE C

Miguel finding lost treasure in the forest.

- ● Miguel found lost treasure in the forest.
- ○ Miguel finding lost treasure. In the forest.
- ○ The way it is

SAMPLE D

Luke wanted to play baseball with his friends.

- ○ Luke wanted to play baseball. With his friends.
- ○ Luke wanting to play baseball with his friends.
- ● The way it is

TIP The group of words that sounds best is the right answer.

5 Black smoke come from the old truck.
- ● Black smoke came from the old truck.
- ○ Black smoke came. From the old truck.
- ○ The way it is

7 The doctor looked. At the bump on Jamal's head.
- ○ The doctor looking at the bump on Jamal's head.
- ● The doctor looked at the bump on Jamal's head.
- ○ The way it is

6 My sister is teaching me to play the piano.
- ○ My sister is teaching me. To play the piano.
- ○ My sister teach me to play the piano.
- ● The way it is

STOP

54

Say In this part of the lesson, read the sentence in the box and the answer choices carefully while I read them aloud. Remember, you are looking for the group of words that is a correct sentence, and the correct answer will sound best to you. It is also important to look carefully at the punctuation in the sentence. In short, the best way to find the correct answers in this lesson is to look and listen carefully.

Say Now you will do more items. Read each sentence in the box to yourself while I read it aloud. Find the answer choice that is the best way to write the sentence or choose *The way it is.* When you mark your answers, make sure you fill in the spaces with dark marks. Do not write anything except your answer choices in your book. Completely erase any marks for answers that you change. Do you have any questions? Let's begin.

Answer any questions the students have. Allow time between items for students to fill in their answers.

Say Put your finger under Number 5 below the samples. "Black smoke come from the old truck." How should the group of words in the box be written? Should it be written *Black smoke came from the old truck. … Black smoke came. From the old truck. …* or should it be written *The way it is?* Mark the space for your answer.

6. Look at Number 6. "My sister is teaching me to play the piano." How should the group of words in the box be written? Should it be written *My sister is teaching me. To play the piano. … My sister teach me to play the piano. …* or should it be written *The way it is?* Mark the space for your answer.

7. Look at Number 7. "The doctor looked. At the bump on Jamal's head." How should the group of words in the box be written? Should it be written *The doctor looking at the bump on Jamal's head. … The doctor looked at the bump on Jamal's head. …* or should it be written *The way it is?* Mark the space for your answer.

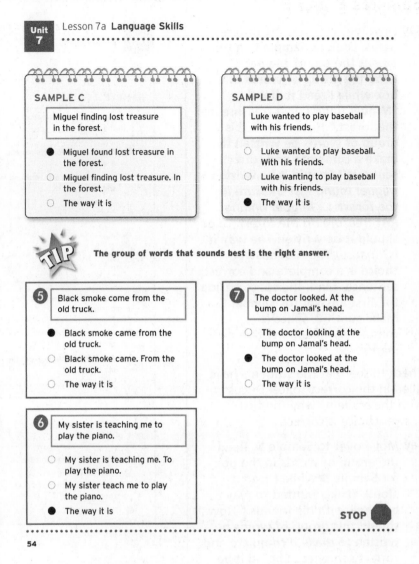

Check to be sure the students have filled in their answer spaces correctly.

Say Look at the next page, page 55.

Check to be sure the students are on the right page.

Samples E and F

Say Now we will do a different kind of item. Find Sample E at the top of the page. Read the question to yourself while I read it aloud. "Terry is writing a story about how her family feeds birds. She wants to organize her ideas before she writes." Should she *Buy a new pencil … Make an outline …* or *Think of a funny story? (pause)* The second answer choice, *Make an outline,* is correct. Mark the space beside the second answer for Sample E. Make sure the space is completely filled in with a dark mark.

Check to see that the students have marked the correct space.

Say Move down to Sample F. Read the question to yourself while I read it aloud. "Eddie is writing a report about electricity. What should he do to get more ideas?" Should he *Read about electricity in an encyclopedia … Turn on a light in his house …* or *Ask his friends if they have a flashlight? (pause)* The first answer choice, *Read about electricity in an encyclopedia,* is correct. Mark the space beside the first answer for Sample F. Make sure the space is completely filled in with a dark mark.

Check to see that the students have marked the correct space.

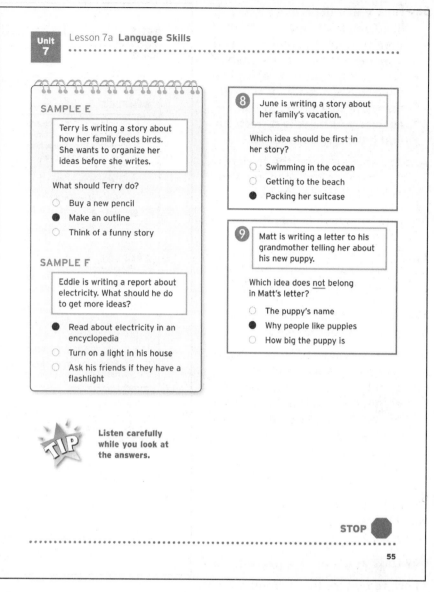

★TIP

Say Now let's look at the tip.

Read the tip aloud to the students.

Say When you answer the questions in this part of the lesson, you should listen carefully while you look at the answers. Choose the answer that makes the most sense with the question. You might ask yourself this question: What would I do if I were writing this?

Say Now you will do more items like Samples E and F. I will read the sentence, the question, and the answer choices aloud while you read to yourself. When I have finished reading, you will mark the space next to the answer you think is correct. Do you have any questions?

Answer any questions the students have. Allow time between items for students to fill in their answers.

Say Find Number 8 beside the samples. "June is writing a story about her family's vacation. Which idea should be first in her story?" Is it *Swimming in the ocean … Getting to the beach …* or *Packing her suitcase?* Mark the space for your answer.

9. Move down to Number 9. "Matt is writing a letter to his grandmother telling her about his new puppy. Which idea does <u>not</u> belong in Matt's letter?" The answers are *The puppy's name … Why people like puppies … How big the puppy is.* Mark your answer.

Check to be sure the students have filled in their answer spaces correctly.

Say Look at the next page, page 56.

Check to be sure the students are on the right page.

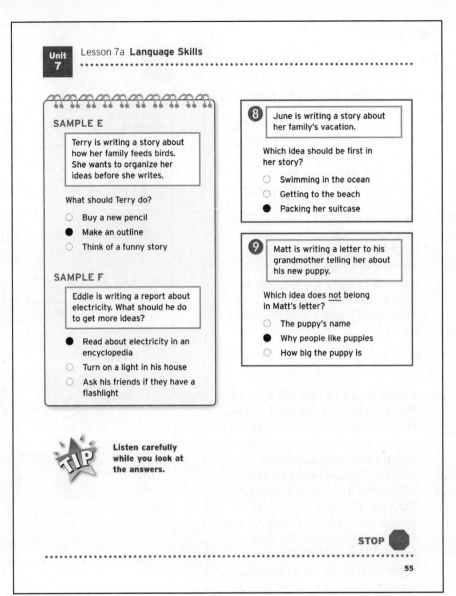

Sample G

Say Look at Sample G at the top of the page. Follow along as I read the paragraph for Sample G. After we read it, you will answer a question about the story.

"Last summer, my family went on a camping trip. We slept in a big tent. One night, Mom heard a noise outside the tent. We all listened quietly. My Dad said it was a bear! The bear was looking for something to eat."

Now look at the question. Read the question to yourself while I read it aloud. "Which of these would go <u>best</u> after the last sentence?" *I remember reading "Goldilocks and the Three Bears." ... The bear went away when it found nothing to eat. ... The tent was green and had a window in back.* Which answer is correct? *(pause)* The second answer is correct because it fits best with the rest of the story. The other answer choices are about a story and the tent. Fill in the second answer space for Sample G. Check to make sure your answer space is completely filled in with a dark mark.

Check to see that the students have filled in the correct answer space.

Discuss with the students why the second answer for Sample G is correct and the other answers are wrong because they are not about the paragraph.

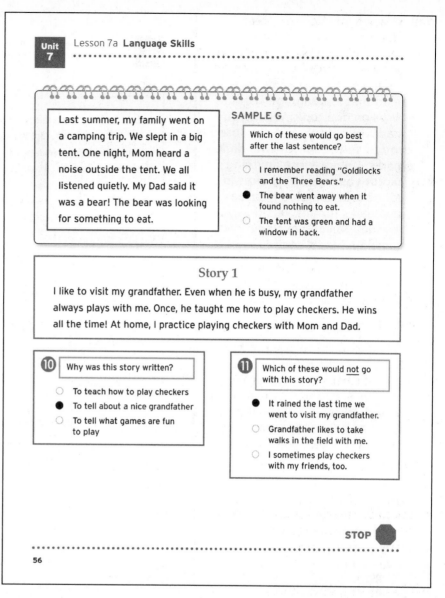

Say Now we will do more items together. I will read the paragraph and questions aloud while you follow along silently. When you do the items, keep in mind that a paragraph should focus on one topic. When you mark your answers, make sure you fill in the spaces with dark marks. Do not write anything except your answer choices in your book. Completely erase any marks for answers that you change. Do you have any questions? Let's begin.

Answer any questions the students have. Allow time between items for the students to fill in their answers.

Say Read along as I read Story 1.

"I like to visit my grandfather. Even when he is busy, my grandfather always plays with me. Once, he taught me how to play checkers. He wins all the time! At home, I practice playing checkers with Mom and Dad."

10. Look at Number 10. "Why was this story written?" *To teach how to play checkers … To tell about a nice grandfather … To tell what games are fun to play.* Mark your answer.

11. Move over to Number 11. "Which of these would not go with this story?" *It rained the last time we went to visit my grandfather. … Grandfather likes to take walks in the field with me. … I sometimes play checkers with my friends, too.* Mark your answer.

Say It's time to stop. You have finished Lesson 7a.

Review the answers with the students. If any items caused particular difficulty, work through them with the students.

Have the students indicate completion of the lesson by entering their score for this activity on the progress chart at the beginning of the book. Provide the students whatever help is necessary to record their scores.

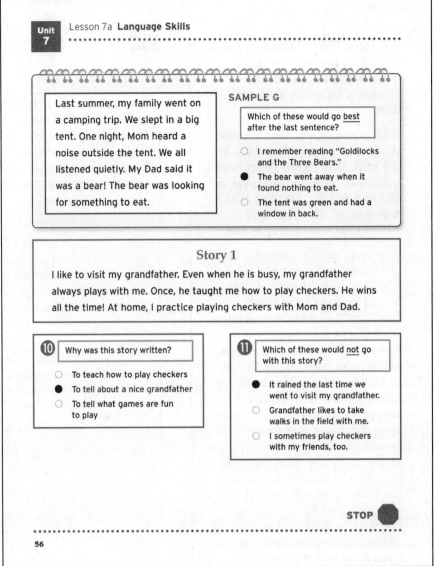

Unit 7   Lesson 7a **Language Skills**

Last summer, my family went on a camping trip. We slept in a big tent. One night, Mom heard a noise outside the tent. We all listened quietly. My Dad said it was a bear! The bear was looking for something to eat.

SAMPLE G

Which of these would go best after the last sentence?

○ I remember reading "Goldilocks and the Three Bears."
● The bear went away when it found nothing to eat.
○ The tent was green and had a window in back.

Story 1

I like to visit my grandfather. Even when he is busy, my grandfather always plays with me. Once, he taught me how to play checkers. He wins all the time! At home, I practice playing checkers with Mom and Dad.

10 Why was this story written?

○ To teach how to play checkers
● To tell about a nice grandfather
○ To tell what games are fun to play

11 Which of these would not go with this story?

● It rained the last time we went to visit my grandfather.
○ Grandfather likes to take walks in the field with me.
○ I sometimes play checkers with my friends, too.

STOP

56

Unit 7 · Lesson 7b Language Skills

Focus

Language Skills
- identifying correct capitalization
- identifying correct punctuation
- choosing correctly used words
- identifying correctly formed sentences
- identifying the best sentence to add to a paragraph
- identifying the main reason for a paragraph
- identifying a sentence that does not fit in a paragraph

Test-taking Skills
- working methodically
- staying with the first answer
- indicating that an item has no mistakes
- listening carefully
- using context to find the answer
- referring to a passage to answer questions

Samples A and B

Say Turn to Lesson 7b on page 57. The page number is at the bottom of the page on the right.

Check to see that the students have found the right page.

Say In this lesson, you will answer more questions about written English. When you answer a question, mark the space for the answer you think is right. Be sure your answer space is completely filled in with a dark mark. Find Sample A at the top of the page.

Check to see that the students have found Sample A.

Say Look at Sample A. Read the sentence with the underlined part to yourself while I read it aloud. "My orange cat likes to sit in my <u>lap.</u>" How should the underlined part be written? Should it be *lap* followed by a question mark ... *lap* followed by an exclamation mark ... or should it be written *The way it is?*

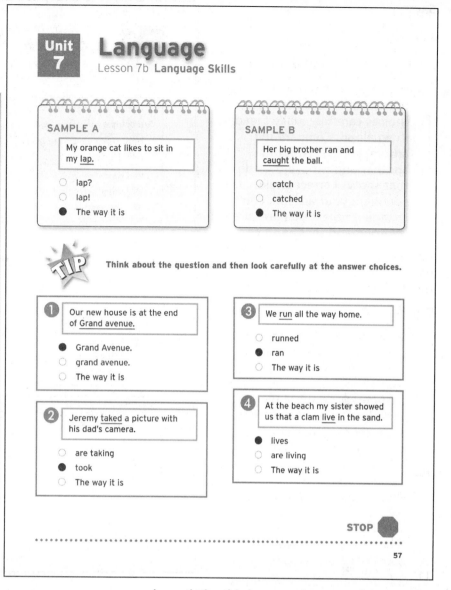

(pause) The third answer is correct because the underlined part is correct *The way it is.* Mark the space beside the third answer for Sample A. Make sure the space is completely filled in with a dark mark.

Check to see that the students have marked the correct space.

Say Now do Sample B. Read the sentence with the underlined part to yourself while I read it aloud. "Her big brother ran and <u>caught</u> the ball." How should the underlined part be written? Should it be *catch ... catched ...* or should it be written *The way it is? (pause)* The underlined part is correct, so you should mark the space beside the last answer, *The way it is.* Make sure the space is completely filled in with a dark mark.

Check to see that the students have filled in the correct answer space.

Say Now let's look at the tip.

Read the tip aloud to the students.

Say It is important that you look at the sentence and the answer choices carefully while I read them aloud. Compare the answer choices with one another and choose the one that shows correct English. Once you mark your answer, don't change it unless you are sure it is wrong and that another choice is better. More often than not, your first answer is correct.

Practice

Say Now you will do more items. Listen carefully to what I say. If there is an error, find the answer choice that shows the correct way to write the underlined part. If there is no error, choose the last answer choice, *The way it is.* Make sure you fill in the spaces with dark marks. Do not write anything except your answer choices in your book. Completely erase any marks for answers that you change. Do you have any questions? Let's begin.

Answer any questions the students have. Allow time between items for students to fill in their answers.

Say Put your finger under Number 1 below the samples. "Our new house is at the end of <u>Grand avenue.</u>" How should the underlined part of the sentence be written? Look carefully at the capitalization of the answer choices and then mark your answer.

2. Move down to Number 2. "Jeremy <u>taked</u> a picture with his dad's camera." How should the underlined part of the sentence be written? Should it be *are taking ... took ...* or *The way it is?* Mark your answer.

3. Move over to Number 3. "We <u>run</u> all the way home." How should the underlined part of the sentence be written? Should it be *runned ... ran ...* or *The way it is?* Mark your answer.

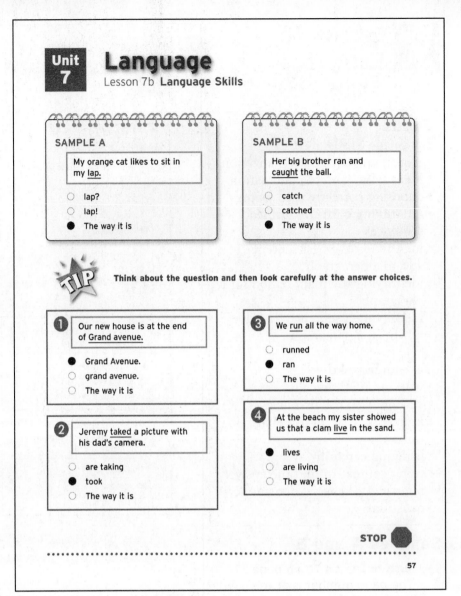

4. Move down to Number 4. "At the beach my sister showed us that a clam <u>live</u> in the sand." How should the underlined part of the sentence be written? Should it be *lives ... are living ...* or should it be written *The way it is?* Mark the space for your answer.

Check to be sure the students have filled in their answer spaces correctly.

Say Look at the next page, page 58.

Check to be sure the students are on the right page.

Samples C and D

Say Now we will do some different items. Look at Sample C in the box at the top of the page. Read the group of words in the box while I read it aloud. "My pet turtle likes to eat. A lot of food." How should this group of words be written to make a complete and correct sentence? Should it be written *My pet turtle like to eat a lot of food.* … *My pet turtle likes to eat a lot of food.* … or should it be written *The way it is?* (pause) The second answer choice is a complete and correct sentence. Mark the space beside the second answer for Sample C. Make sure the space is completely filled in with a dark mark.

Check to see that the students have filled in the correct space. Discuss with the students why the second answer choice is correct.

Say Move over to Sample D. Read the group of words in the box for Sample D while I read it aloud. "My sister wanted to play with her friends all day." How should this group of words be written to make a complete and correct sentence? Should it be written *My sister wanted to play. With her friends all day.* … *My sister wanting to play with her friends all day.* … or should it be written *The way it is?* (pause) The last answer choice is correct because the group of words in the box is a complete and correct sentence. Mark the space beside the last answer for Sample D. Make sure the space is completely filled in with a dark mark.

Check to see that the students have filled in the correct answer space.

Say Now you will do more items. Read each sentence in the box to yourself while I read it aloud. Find the answer choice that is the best way to write the sentence or choose *The way it is.* When you mark your answers, make sure you fill in the spaces with dark marks. Do not write anything except your answer choices in your book. Completely erase any marks for answers that you change. Do you have any questions? Let's begin.

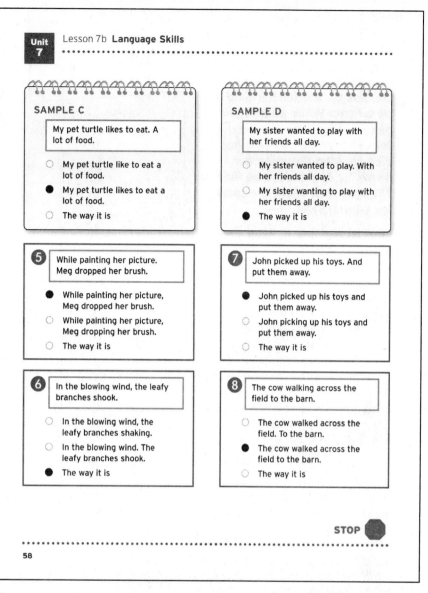

Answer any questions the students have. Allow time between items for students to fill in their answers.

Say Put your finger under Number 5 below the samples. "While painting her picture. Meg dropped her brush." How should the group of words in the box be written? Should it be written *While painting her picture, Meg dropped her brush. … While painting her picture, Meg dropping her brush. …* or should it be written *The way it is?* Mark the space for your answer.

6. Look at Number 6. Read the group of words in the box while I read it aloud. "In the blowing wind, the leafy branches shook." How should the group of words in the box be written? Should it be written *In the blowing wind, the leafy branches shaking.* like the first answer … *In the blowing wind. The leafy branches shook.* like the second answer … or should it be written *The way it is?* Mark the space for your answer.

7. Look at Number 7. Read the group of words in the box while I read it aloud. "John picked up his toys. And put them away." How should the group of words in the box be written? Should it be written *John picked up his toys and put them away.* like the first answer … *John picking up his toys and put them away.* like the second answer … or should it be written *The way it is?* Mark the space for your answer.

8. Look at Number 8. Read the group of words in the box while I read it aloud. "The cow walking across the field to the barn." How should the group of words in the box be written? Should it be written *The cow walked across the field. To the barn. … The cow walked across the field to the barn. …* or should it be written *The way it is?* Mark the space for your answer.

Check to be sure the students have filled in their answer spaces correctly.

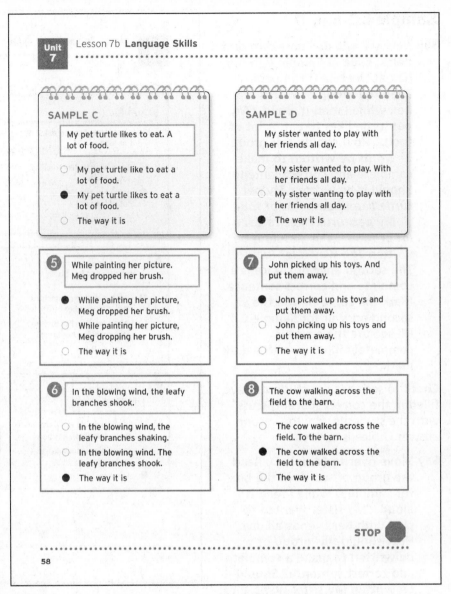

Say Look at the next page, page 59.

Check to be sure the students are on the right page.

Sample E

Say Look at Sample E at the top of the page. Follow along as I read the paragraph for Sample E. After we read it, you will answer a question about the story.

"Mrs. Sanchez stirred a jar of water as she added sugar. When the sugar disappeared, she poured the sugar water into a red container. 'What are you making?' asked Pablo. 'This is food for hummingbirds,' she answered. 'Do you want to help me feed them?'"

Now look at the question. Read the question to yourself while I read it aloud. "Which of these would go <u>best</u> after the last sentence?" The answers are *Pablo smiled and said, "That would be fun!" … Mrs. Sanchez dried her hands on the towel. … Pablo went outside to play with his friends.* Which answer is correct? *(pause)* The first answer is correct because it makes the most sense with the rest of the paragraph. Fill in the first answer space for Sample E. Check to make sure your answer space is completely filled in with a dark mark.

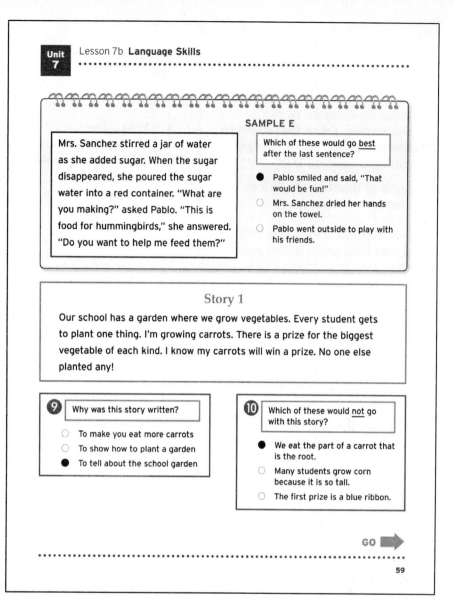

Check to see that the students have filled in the correct answer space. Be sure the students understand why the first answer is correct.

Say Now we will do more items. I will read the paragraph and questions aloud while you follow along silently. When you do the items, keep in mind that a paragraph should focus on one topic. When you mark your answers, make sure you fill in the spaces with dark marks. Do not write anything except your answer choices in your book. Completely erase any marks for answers that you change. Do you have any questions? Let's begin.

Answer any questions the students have. Allow time between items for the students to fill in their answers.

Say Read along as I read Story 1.

"Our school has a garden where we grow vegetables. Every student gets to plant one thing. I'm growing carrots. There is a prize for the biggest vegetable of each kind. I know my carrots will win a prize. No one else planted any!"

9. Look at Number 9. "Why was this story written?" *To make you eat more carrots … To show how to plant a garden … To tell about the school garden.* Mark your answer.

10. Look at Number 10. "Which of these would <u>not</u> go with this story?" *We eat the part of a carrot that is the root. … Many students grow corn because it is so tall. … The first prize is a blue ribbon.* Mark your answer.

Look at the next page, page 60.

Check to be sure the students are on the right page.

Say Read along as I read Story 2.

"Jenna and her family live near a warm beach. She had never seen snow except in pictures. During the winter break, Jenna went on vacation to the mountains. Jenna was going to see real snow. She was even going to learn to ski!"

11. Look at Number 11. "Which of these would not go with this story?" *Jenna loved the snow, but thought it was very cold. ... Jenna likes other sports better than skiing. ... Jenna had to borrow ski clothes from her friends.* Mark your answer.

12. Look at Number 12. "Why was this story written?" *To tell about Jenna's vacation ... To teach people how to ski ... To show how warm the beach is.* Mark your answer.

13. Look at Number 13. "Which of these would go best after the last sentence?" *It has to be cold to snow. ... Jenna knew this trip would be wonderful. ... Many people take their vacation during the summer.* Mark your answer.

It's time to stop. You have finished Lesson 7b.

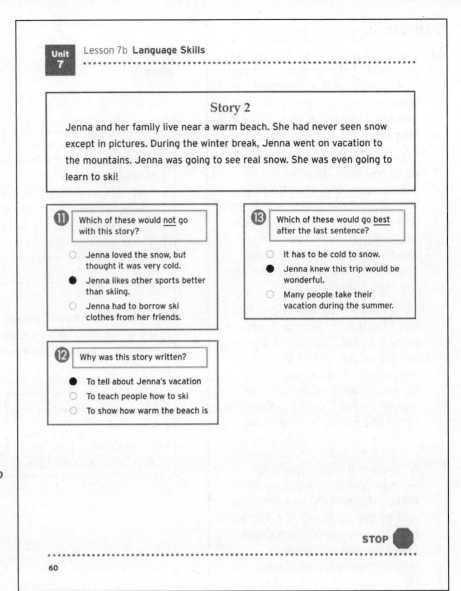

Unit 7 Lesson 7b **Language Skills**

Story 2

Jenna and her family live near a warm beach. She had never seen snow except in pictures. During the winter break, Jenna went on vacation to the mountains. Jenna was going to see real snow. She was even going to learn to ski!

11 Which of these would not go with this story?
- ○ Jenna loved the snow, but thought it was very cold.
- ● Jenna likes other sports better than skiing.
- ○ Jenna had to borrow ski clothes from her friends.

13 Which of these would go best after the last sentence?
- ○ It has to be cold to snow.
- ● Jenna knew this trip would be wonderful.
- ○ Many people take their vacation during the summer.

12 Why was this story written?
- ● To tell about Jenna's vacation
- ○ To teach people how to ski
- ○ To show how warm the beach is

STOP

60

Review the answers with the students. If any items caused particular difficulty, work through them with the students. You may find it helpful to discuss the items to be sure the students understand what they are supposed to do.

Have the students indicate completion of the lesson by entering their score for this activity on the progress chart at the beginning of the book. Provide the students whatever help is necessary to record their scores.

Unit 7 Test Yourself: Language

Focus

Language Skills
- identifying correct capitalization
- identifying correct punctuation
- choosing correctly used words
- identifying correctly formed sentences
- identifying the main reason for a paragraph
- identifying the best sentence to add to a paragraph
- identifying a sentence that does not fit in a paragraph

Test-taking Skills
- listening carefully
- marking the right answer as soon as it is found
- indicating that an item has no mistakes
- comparing answer choices
- subvocalizing answer choices
- working methodically
- staying with the first answer
- using context to find the answer
- referring to a passage to answer questions

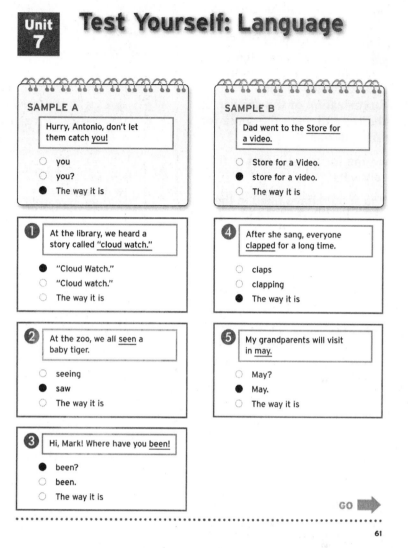

This lesson simulates an actual test-taking experience. Therefore, it is recommended that the directions be read verbatim and the suggested procedures be followed.

Directions

Administration Time: approximately 50 minutes

Say Turn to the Test Yourself lesson on page 61.

Check to be sure the students have found the right page. Point out to the students that this is not a real test and that they will score it themselves to see how well they are doing. Encourage the students to avoid spending too much time on any one item and to take the best guess if they are unsure of the answer.

Say There are different types of items in the Test Yourself lesson, so you will have to pay close attention to what I say. Remember to make sure that the spaces for your answers are

completely filled in. Press your pencil firmly so that your marks come out dark. Completely erase any marks for answers that you change.

Find Sample A at the top of the page. Read the sentence with the underlined part to yourself while I read it aloud. "Hurry, Antonio, don't let them catch you!" How should the underlined part be written? Look carefully at the punctuation of the answers. Mark the space for your answer.

Allow time for the students to fill in their answers.

Say You should have filled in the space next to the third answer because the underlined part is correct *The way it is.* If you chose another answer, erase yours and fill in the third space now.

Check to see that the students have marked the correct space.

Say Now do Sample B. Read the sentence with the underlined part to yourself while I read it aloud. "Dad went to the Store for a video." How should the underlined part be written? Look carefully at the capitalization of the answer choices and mark the space for your answer.

Allow time for the students to fill in their answers.

Say You should have filled in the space beside the second answer. If you chose another answer, erase yours and fill in the second space now.

Check to see that the students have marked the correct space.

Say Now you will do more items like the samples. Read the items to yourself while I read them aloud.

Allow time between items for the students to fill in their answers.

Say Put your finger under Number 1. "At the library, we heard a story called 'cloud watch.'" How should the underlined part be written? Look very closely at the capitalization and punctuation and then mark your answer.

2. Move down to Number 2. "At the zoo, we all <u>seen</u> a baby tiger." How should the underlined part be written? Should it be *seeing ... saw ...* or should it be written *The way it is*? Mark your answer.

3. Move down to Number 3. "Hi, Mark! Where have you <u>been!</u>" Look very closely at the punctuation of the answer choices and then mark your answer.

4. Look at Number 4. "After she sang, everyone <u>clapped</u> for a long time." How should the underlined part be written? Should it be *claps ... clapping ...* or should it be written *The way it is*? Mark your answer.

5. Move down to Number 5. "My grandparents will visit in <u>may.</u>" Look very closely at the punctuation and capitalization of the answer choices and then mark your answer.

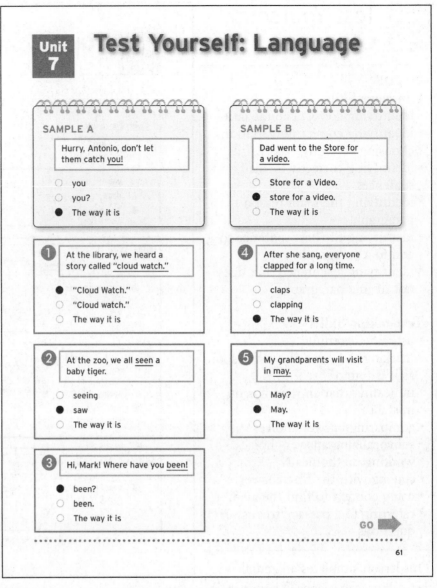

| Unit 7 | **Test Yourself: Language** |

SAMPLE A

Hurry, Antonio, don't let them catch <u>you!</u>

- ○ you
- ○ you?
- ● The way it is

SAMPLE B

Dad went to the <u>Store for a video.</u>

- ○ Store for a Video.
- ● store for a video.
- ○ The way it is

1 At the library, we heard a story called <u>"cloud watch."</u>

- ● "Cloud Watch."
- ○ "Cloud watch."
- ○ The way it is

2 At the zoo, we all <u>seen</u> a baby tiger.

- ○ seeing
- ● saw
- ○ The way it is

3 Hi, Mark! Where have you <u>been!</u>

- ● been?
- ○ been.
- ○ The way it is

4 After she sang, everyone <u>clapped</u> for a long time.

- ○ claps
- ○ clapping
- ● The way it is

5 My grandparents will visit in <u>may.</u>

- ○ May?
- ● May.
- ○ The way it is

GO ➡

61

Say Look at the next page, page 62.

Check to be sure the students are on the right page.

Say Put your finger under Number 6 at the top of the page. "For dinner, <u>Tom maked</u> some pizza." How should the underlined part be written? Should it be *Tom made* with a capital T … *tom maked* with a small t … or should it be written *The way it is?* Mark your answer.

7. Move down to Number 7. "We live near the <u>Bay bridge.</u>" How should the underlined part be written? Look carefully at the capitalization and punctuation of the answer choices. Mark your answer.

8. Move down to Number 8. "They moved here from <u>Omaha Nebraska.</u>" How should the underlined part be written? Look carefully at the punctuation and capitalization. Mark your answer.

9. Move down to Number 9. "Can you guess how tall I <u>am?</u>" How should the underlined part be written? Look very closely at the capitalization and punctuation and then mark your answer.

10. Look at Number 10 in the next column. "She was very quiet <u>that Night.</u>" Look carefully at the capitalization and punctuation. Mark your answer.

11. Move down to Number 11. "I saw a <u>Movie with Ellen.</u>" How should the underlined part be written? Look very closely at the capitalization and punctuation and then mark your answer.

12. Move down to Number 12. "I was eight when we <u>move</u> to Texas." How should the underlined part be written? Should it be *moved … is moving …* or *The way it is?* Mark your answer.

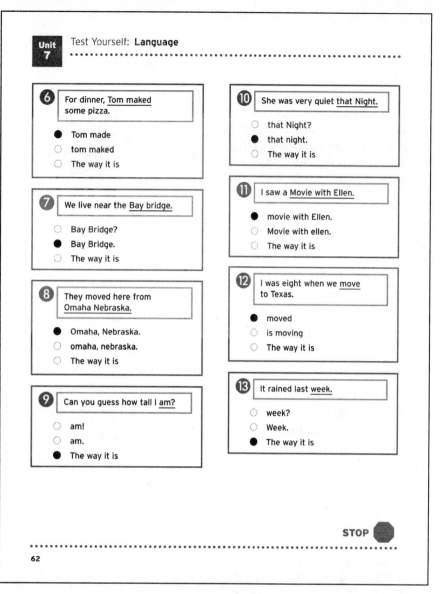

13. Move down to Number 13. "It rained last <u>week.</u>" How should the underlined part be written? Look very closely at the capitalization and punctuation and then mark your answer.

Look at the next page, page 63.

Check to be sure the students are on the right page. Allow the students a moment to rest.

Say Look at Sample C at the top of the page. Read the group of words in the box while I read it aloud. "A rooster crows every day at dawn." How should this group of words be written to make a complete and correct sentence? Should it be written *A rooster crows. Every day at dawn. … A rooster crows every day. At dawn. …* or is it correct *The way it is?* Mark your answer.

Allow time for the students to fill in their answers.

Say The space beside the last answer should be filled in because the sentence in the box is correct *The way it is.* If you chose another answer, erase yours and fill in the last space now.

Check to see that the students have filled in the correct answer space.

Say Find Sample D at the top of the page on the right. Read the group of words in the box while I read it aloud. "Kittens drinking milk from a bowl on the floor." How should this group of words be written to make a complete and correct sentence? Should it be written *Kittens drank milk. From a bowl on the floor. … Kittens drank milk from a bowl on the floor. …* or is the group of words correct *The way it is?* Mark your answer.

Allow time for the students to fill in their answers.

Say The space for the second answer should be filled in. If you chose another answer, erase yours and fill in the second space now.

Check to see that the students have filled in the correct answer space.

Say Now we will do more items like Samples C and D. Read each sentence in the box to yourself while I read it aloud. Find the answer choice that is the best way to write the sentence or choose *The way it is.* Let's begin.

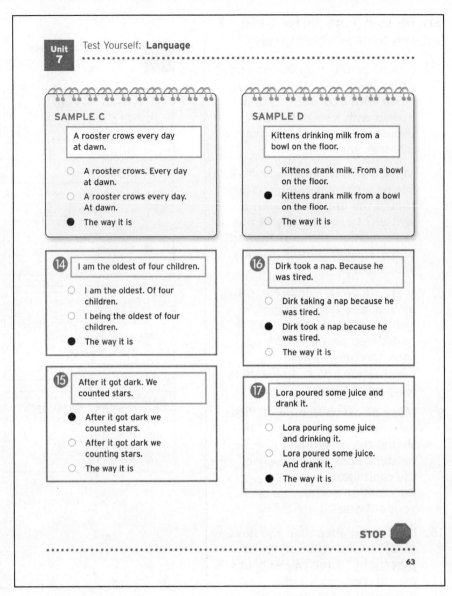

SAMPLE C

A rooster crows every day at dawn.

○ A rooster crows. Every day at dawn.
○ A rooster crows every day. At dawn.
● The way it is

SAMPLE D

Kittens drinking milk from a bowl on the floor.

○ Kittens drank milk. From a bowl on the floor.
● Kittens drank milk from a bowl on the floor.
○ The way it is

14 I am the oldest of four children.

○ I am the oldest. Of four children.
○ I being the oldest of four children.
● The way it is

16 Dirk took a nap. Because he was tired.

○ Dirk taking a nap because he was tired.
● Dirk took a nap because he was tired.
○ The way it is

15 After it got dark. We counted stars.

● After it got dark we counted stars.
○ After it got dark we counting stars.
○ The way it is

17 Lora poured some juice and drank it.

○ Lora pouring some juice and drinking it.
○ Lora poured some juice. And drank it.
● The way it is

STOP

63

Allow time between items for the students to fill in their answers.

Say Find Number 14 below the samples. Read the group of words in the box while I read it aloud. "I am the oldest of four children." How should the group of words in the box be written? Should it be written *I am the oldest. Of four children.* … *I being the oldest of four children.* … or should it be written *The way it is?* Mark the space for your answer.

15. Move down to Number 15. Read the group of words in the box while I read it aloud. "After it got dark. We counted stars." How should the group of words in the box be written? Should it be written *After it got dark we counted stars.* … *After it got dark we counting stars.* … or should it be written *The way it is?* Mark the space for your answer.

16. Move over to Number 16 in the second column. Read the group of words in the box while I read it aloud. "Dirk took a nap. Because he was tired." How should the group of words in the box be written? Should it be written *Dirk taking a nap because he was tired.* … *Dirk took a nap because he was tired.* … or should it be written *The way it is?* Mark the space for your answer.

17. Move down to Number 17. Read the group of words in the box while I read it aloud. "Lora poured some juice and drank it." How should the group of words in the box be written? Should it be written *Lora pouring some juice and drinking it.* … *Lora poured some juice. And drank it.* … or should it be written *The way it is?* Mark the space for your answer.

    Look at the next page, page 64.

Check to be sure the students are on the right page. Allow the students a moment to rest.

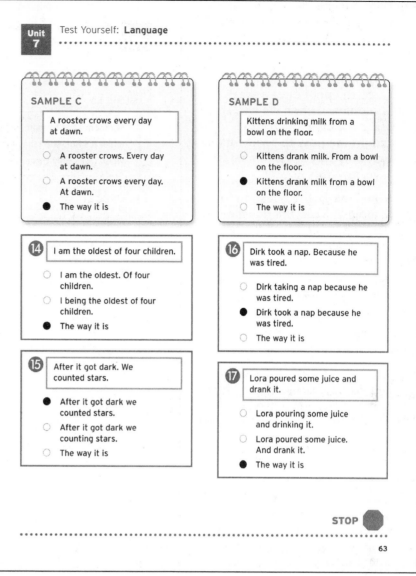

Say Let's do Samples E and F at the top of the page. Follow along as I read the paragraph for the samples.

"My mom likes to swim, so we go to the pool once a week. Sometimes, when it's hot, she takes me every day. Mom taught me how to swim when I was only three. Swimming is my favorite sport now."

Now look at the question for Sample E. Read the question to yourself while I read it aloud. "Why was this story written?" *To tell how big the pool is … To explain how to swim … To tell about swimming.* Mark the space for your answer.

Allow time for the students to fill in their answers.

Say The space for the last answer should be filled in. If you chose another answer, erase yours and fill in the last answer space now.

Check to see that the students have filled in the correct answer space.

Now look at the question for Sample F. Read the question to yourself while I read it aloud. "Which of these would go <u>best</u> after the last sentence?" The answers are *It gets really hot in the summer. … I hope to be in the Olympics someday. … Sometimes the water is cold at first.* Mark the space for your answer.

Allow time for the students to fill in their answers.

Say The space for the second answer should be filled in. If you chose another answer, erase yours and fill in the second answer space now.

Check to see that the students have filled in the correct answer space.

Look at the next page, page 65.

Check to be sure the students are on the right page. Allow the students a moment to rest.

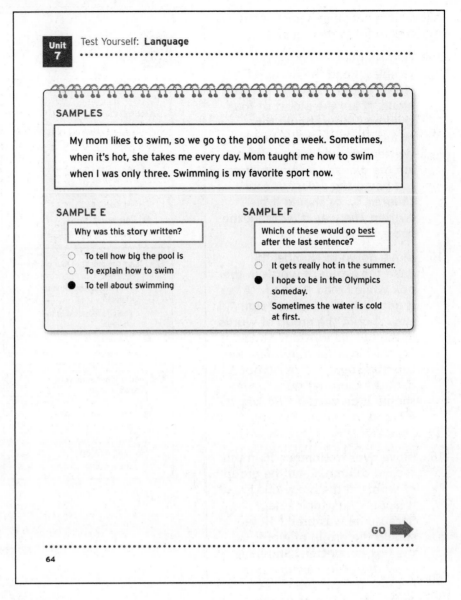

SAMPLES

My mom likes to swim, so we go to the pool once a week. Sometimes, when it's hot, she takes me every day. Mom taught me how to swim when I was only three. Swimming is my favorite sport now.

SAMPLE E

Why was this story written?

○ To tell how big the pool is
○ To explain how to swim
● To tell about swimming

SAMPLE F

Which of these would go <u>best</u> after the last sentence?

○ It gets really hot in the summer.
● I hope to be in the Olympics someday.
○ Sometimes the water is cold at first.

GO ➡

64

Say Now you will do more items. Listen carefully to what I say while you read the paragraphs and the items to yourself. Choose the answer you think is best. Let's begin.

Allow time between items for the students to fill in their answers.

Say Read along as I read Story 1.

"Yesterday was a special day at our house. We took my little brother to the library. He was getting his first library card, and he was very excited. It took him a long time to pick out a book."

18. Look at Number 18. "Which of these would go **best** after the last sentence?" *The name of his book is "Mr. Fish Runs the School." ... Our library is a big building, all the way downtown. ... Sometimes we get to take out videos at the library, too.* Mark your answer.

19. Look at Number 19. "Which of these does **not** go with the story?" *My brother just learned to read. ... You must return books to the library. ... He asked me to help him read the book.* Mark your answer.

Look at the next page, page 66.

Check to be sure the students are on the right page.

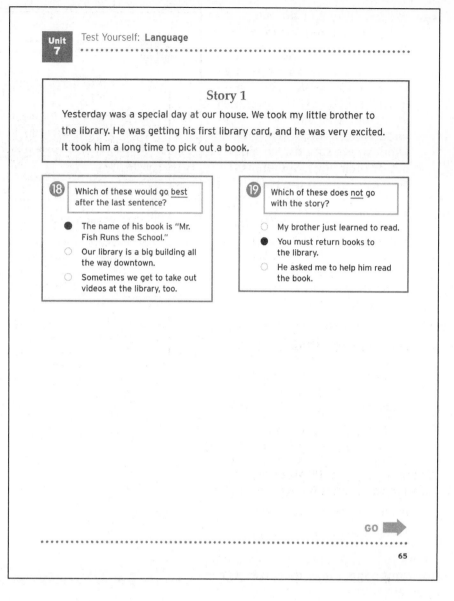

Story 1

Yesterday was a special day at our house. We took my little brother to the library. He was getting his first library card, and he was very excited. It took him a long time to pick out a book.

18 Which of these would go <u>best</u> after the last sentence?

● The name of his book is "Mr. Fish Runs the School."

○ Our library is a big building all the way downtown.

○ Sometimes we get to take out videos at the library, too.

19 Which of these does <u>not</u> go with the story?

○ My brother just learned to read.

● You must return books to the library.

○ He asked me to help him read the book.

GO

65

Say Look at Story 2 at the top of the page. Read along as I read the story.

"My family went on a trip to a nature museum. We saw shells, rocks, and insects. The best part of the museum was underwater! Through a window, we saw fish coming out of their eggs. Sometimes they got stuck in the rocks."

20. Look at Number 20. "Which of these would go <u>best</u> after the last sentence?" *They had to wiggle to get loose. … We didn't get to see any ducks. … I once saw a chicken egg hatch.* Mark your answer.

21. Look at Number 21. "Why was this story written?" *To tell where fish come from … To explain about shells and rocks … To tell about a special trip.* Mark the space for your answer.

22. Look at Number 22. "Which of these would <u>not</u> go with this story?" *My parents like to take us to museums. … Fishing is my favorite hobby. … Some of the insects were really strange.*

Look at the next page, page 67.

Check to be sure the students are on the right page. Allow the students a moment to rest.

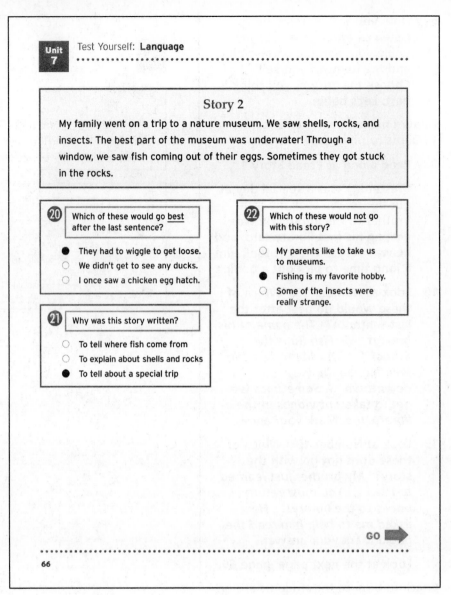

Story 2

My family went on a trip to a nature museum. We saw shells, rocks, and insects. The best part of the museum was underwater! Through a window, we saw fish coming out of their eggs. Sometimes they got stuck in the rocks.

20. Which of these would go <u>best</u> after the last sentence?
● They had to wiggle to get loose.
○ We didn't get to see any ducks.
○ I once saw a chicken egg hatch.

21. Why was this story written?
○ To tell where fish come from
○ To explain about shells and rocks
● To tell about a special trip

22. Which of these would <u>not</u> go with this story?
○ My parents like to take us to museums.
● Fishing is my favorite hobby.
○ Some of the insects were really strange.

GO ➡

66

Say Look at Story 3 at the top of the page. Read along as I read the story.

"Carly likes building sandcastles at the beach. She spends most of her summer days building with sand. Small boxes and cups help shape the sand into castle walls. An old spoon is perfect for digging paths, tunnels, and doorways. "

23. Put your finger under the question for Number 23. "Which of these would go <u>best</u> at the end of this story?" *Sand castle building is done all over the world. ... Summer vacation lasts from June to September. ... Carly hopes to win a sand castle contest someday.* Mark the space for your answer.

24. Move down to Number 24. "Which of these does <u>not</u> belong in this story?" *Carly's parents once visited a real castle. ... People stop to stare at Carly's sand castles. ... Carly's sand castles are over two feet tall.* Mark your answer.

25. Look at Number 25. "Why was this story written?" *To tell about living in a castle ... To tell what old castles are made of ... To tell what Carly does in the summer.* Mark your answer.

Turn to the next page, page 68.

Check to be sure the students are on the right page.

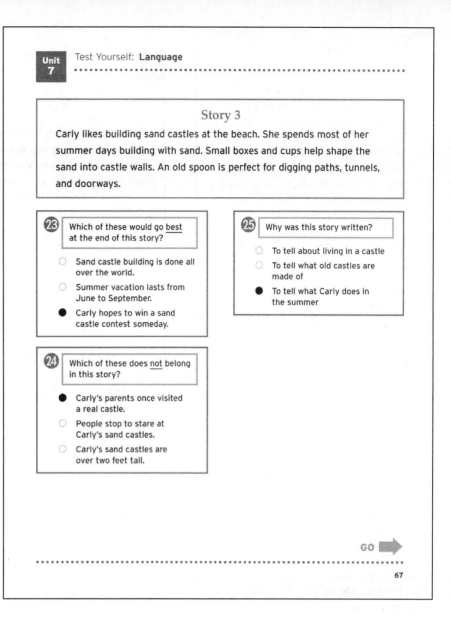

Story 3

Carly likes building sand castles at the beach. She spends most of her summer days building with sand. Small boxes and cups help shape the sand into castle walls. An old spoon is perfect for digging paths, tunnels, and doorways.

23. Which of these would go <u>best</u> at the end of this story?
   ○ Sand castle building is done all over the world.
   ○ Summer vacation lasts from June to September.
   ● Carly hopes to win a sand castle contest someday.

24. Which of these does <u>not</u> belong in this story?
   ● Carly's parents once visited a real castle.
   ○ People stop to stare at Carly's sand castles.
   ○ Carly's sand castles are over two feet tall.

25. Why was this story written?
   ○ To tell about living in a castle
   ○ To tell what old castles are made of
   ● To tell what Carly does in the summer

GO

67

Say Look at Story 4 at the top of the page. Read along as I read the story aloud.

"Today, we learned how to paint a sunset. First, we took a sponge and made our paper very wet. Across the middle, we painted yellow and red stripes. Then, we painted dark blue across the top. Finally, we used the wet sponge to blend the stripes together."

26. Look at Number 26. "Why was this story written?" *To tell how to paint a sunset ... To describe a sunset ... To teach about all the colors.* Mark your answer.

27. Look at Number 27. "Which of these would go <u>best</u> after the last sentence?" *Sometimes after a rainstorm, a sunset looks very pretty. ... When our pictures were dry, we painted trees on them. ... I like to paint almost as much as I like to read.* Mark the space for your answer.

28. Look at Number 28. "Which of these would <u>not</u> go with this story?" *The teacher put our paintings on the wall for our parents to see. ... The red and yellow made orange when they mixed together. ... At home, I have a box of crayons that I use for my drawings.* Mark the space for your answer.

It's time to stop. You have completed the Test Yourself lesson.

Review the answers with the students. Have the students indicate completion of the lesson by entering their score for this activity on the progress chart at the beginning of the book. Provide the students whatever help is necessary to record their scores.

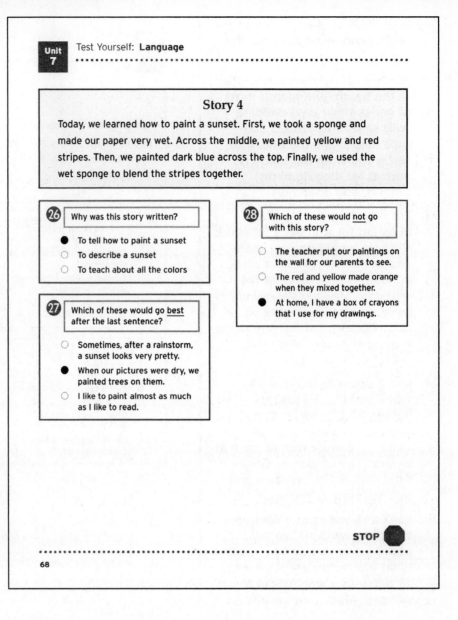

Unit 7 Test Yourself: **Language**

Story 4

Today, we learned how to paint a sunset. First, we took a sponge and made our paper very wet. Across the middle, we painted yellow and red stripes. Then, we painted dark blue across the top. Finally, we used the wet sponge to blend the stripes together.

26 Why was this story written?

● To tell how to paint a sunset
○ To describe a sunset
○ To teach about all the colors

27 Which of these would go **best** after the last sentence?

○ Sometimes, after a rainstorm, a sunset looks very pretty.
● When our pictures were dry, we painted trees on them.
○ I like to paint almost as much as I like to read.

28 Which of these would <u>not</u> go with this story?

○ The teacher put our paintings on the wall for our parents to see.
○ The red and yellow made orange when they mixed together.
● At home, I have a box of crayons that I use for my drawings.

STOP

68

Background

This unit contains three lessons that deal with listening skills. Students answer questions about oral vocabulary or paragraphs that are read to them.

• **In Lessons 8a and 8b,** students answer questions about oral vocabulary statements or paragraphs that are read to them. Students learn the importance of following oral directions, listening carefully, and understanding unusual item formats. They mark the right answer as soon as it is found, choose a picture to answer a question, and stay with the first answer. They refer to a picture to answer questions and take the best guess when unsure of the answer.

• **In the Test Yourself lesson,** the listening and test-taking skills introduced and used in Lessons 8a and 8b are reinforced and presented in a format that gives students the experience of taking an achievement test.

Instructional Objectives

Lesson 8a **Listening Skills**	Given an oral sentence, students identify which of three answer choices means the same as a target word in the sentence.
Lesson 8b **Listening Skills**	
	Given an oral paragraph, students identify which of three pictures is the correct response to an orally presented question about the paragraph.
	Given an oral paragraph, students identify which of three or four answer choices is the correct response to an orally presented question about the paragraph.
Test Yourself	Given questions similar to those in Lessons 8a and 8b, students utilize listening skills and test-taking strategies on achievement-test formats.

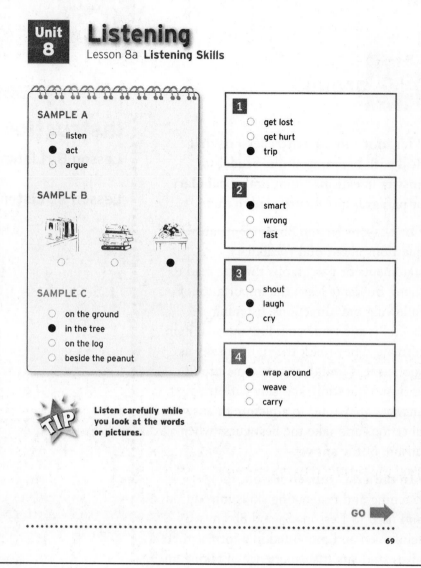

Unit 8

Lesson 8a
Listening Skills

Focus

Listening Skills
- identifying synonyms for orally presented words in context
- choosing a picture to answer questions about an orally presented story
- answering questions about an orally presented story

Test-taking Skills
- following oral directions
- listening carefully
- understanding unusual item formats
- marking the right answer as soon as it is found
- choosing a picture to answer a question

Unit 8

Listening

Lesson 8a **Listening Skills**

SAMPLE A
- ○ listen
- ● act
- ○ argue

SAMPLE B

○ ○ ●

SAMPLE C
- ○ on the ground
- ● in the tree
- ○ on the log
- ○ beside the peanut

1
- ○ get lost
- ○ get hurt
- ● trip

2
- ● smart
- ○ wrong
- ○ fast

3
- ○ shout
- ● laugh
- ○ cry

4
- ● wrap around
- ○ weave
- ○ carry

TIP **Listen carefully while you look at the words or pictures.**

GO

69

Samples A, B, and C

Say Turn to Lesson 8a on page 69. The page number is at the bottom of the page on the right.

Check to see that the students have found the right page.

Say In this lesson, you will answer questions about sentences or stories I read to you. Find Sample A at the top of the page. I will read a sentence. The last part of the sentence will be missing. Then I will read the three answers for the item. You should choose the word that means the same as the word from the sentence. Jenny likes to *perform* in a play. To *perform* is to—*listen* ... *act* ... *argue.* Which word means the same as *perform? (pause)* The correct answer is *act. Act* means the same as *perform.* Mark the space beside *act.* Be sure your answer is filled in with a dark mark.

Check to see that the students have filled in the correct space.

Say Now we'll do Sample B. Look at the three pictures and listen to this story.

A pile of books was on the table. The librarian asked Jay to put the books back on the shelf. Which picture shows how the books were? Were they—*on a shelf* ... *stacked neatly* ... or *in a pile on the table? (pause)* The books were *in a pile on the table.* Mark the last answer space. Press your pencil firmly so your mark comes out dark.

Check to see that the students have marked the correct space.

Say Look at Sample C. I will read a story and ask you a question about it. I will also read the answer choices that are written in your book. Listen carefully.

The bluejay in the tree turned its head and looked at the peanuts on the ground. It flew down and picked one up. Then it flew over to a log and began pecking at the peanut. Soon the jay had opened the peanut and began eating the tasty nuts.

In the beginning of the story the bluejay is—*on the ground … in the tree … on the log … beside the peanut.* Which answer is correct? *(pause)* In the beginning, the bluejay is *in the tree.* Mark the space beside the second answer.

Check to see that the students have marked the correct space.

Say Now let's look at the tip.

Read the tip aloud to the students.

Say It is important that you listen carefully to what I say and look at the words or pictures. As soon as you know which answer is correct, mark your answer and get ready for the next item. If you aren't ready for a question, you will probably choose the wrong answer.

Practice

Say Now you will do more items. They are like the sample items we just did. Listen carefully to what I say as you look at the answer choices. Fill in your answer spaces with dark marks and completely erase any marks for answers that you change. Do you have any questions? Let's begin.

Pause between items to allow time for the students to fill in their answers.

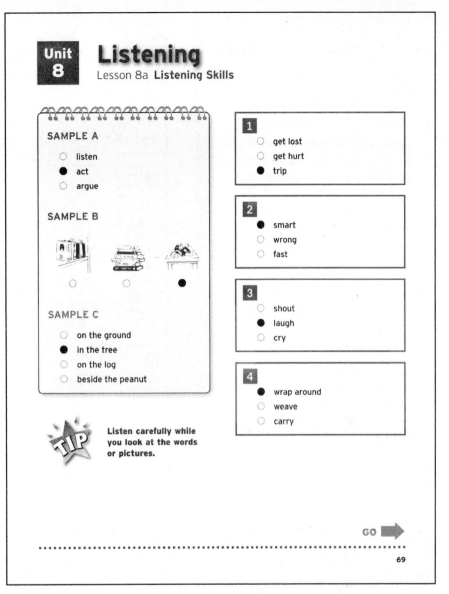

Unit 8 **Listening**
Lesson 8a **Listening Skills**

SAMPLE A
○ listen
● act
○ argue

SAMPLE B

○   ○   ●

SAMPLE C
○ on the ground
● in the tree
○ on the log
○ beside the peanut

TIP
Listen carefully while you look at the words or pictures.

1
○ get lost
○ get hurt
● trip

2
● smart
○ wrong
○ fast

3
○ shout
● laugh
○ cry

4
● wrap around
○ weave
○ carry

GO ➡

69

1. Look at the first group of words beside Sample A. Be careful or you will *stumble. Stumble* means the same as—*get lost … get hurt … trip.*

2. That was a *clever* way to solve the problem. *Clever* means the same as—*smart … wrong … fast.*

3. To giggle is to—*shout … laugh … cry.*

4. Move down to Number 4. Rita will help you *wind* the yarn. *Wind* means about the same as—*wrap around … weave … carry.*

Turn to the next page, page 70.

Check to see that the students have found the right page. Allow time for students to relax.

5. Look at Number 5 at the top of the page. I *gathered* some smooth stones. To *gather* means to—*collect ... throw ... see.*

6. Dad said I needed to *hurry.* Hurry means the same as—*wait ... listen ... rush.*

   Now we will do a different kind of activity. I will read a story and ask you two questions about it. You will choose the picture that is the best answer.

   The Jones family sat around the breakfast table on a lazy Saturday morning. The family was enjoying muffins, juice, and fruit. Everyone was talking about what they would do that day. After they finished eating, Loretta and Nathan helped Mr. Jones with the dishes. Mrs. Jones went to her office beside the kitchen and picked up a letter from the desk. Then she remembered she had to go to the store to get a present for Grandmother's birthday.

7. Move down to Number 7. What did Loretta and Nathan have for breakfast? Was it—*toast and eggs ... muffins ...* or *cereal?* Mark the space for your answer.

8. Look at Number 8. When Mrs. Jones went into her office, she picked up a—*letter ... box of crayons ...* or *present.*

   Look at the answers in the next column.

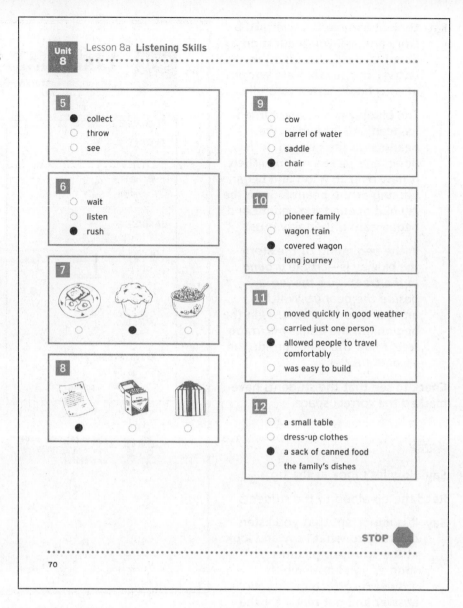

Unit 8   Lesson 8a Listening Skills

5
● collect
○ throw
○ see

6
○ wait
○ listen
● rush

7

8

9
○ cow
○ barrel of water
○ saddle
● chair

10
○ pioneer family
○ wagon train
● covered wagon
○ long journey

11
○ moved quickly in good weather
○ carried just one person
● allowed people to travel comfortably
○ was easy to build

12
○ a small table
○ dress-up clothes
● a sack of canned food
○ the family's dishes

STOP

70

Say Now we will do another activity. I will read a story and ask you four questions about it. I will read the answers aloud while you read along silently. You will choose the answer you think is right. Let's begin.

When the pioneers traveled to the American West, they had to carry everything they needed. They often traveled in covered wagons that could hold many things. Several people rode in the wagon, and inside it were household items like clothes, furniture, and dishes. On the outside of the wagon were tied food, water, and things that were used every day on the trip. A well-loaded wagon would allow the pioneers to travel comfortably. It would also let them carry everything they would need when they arrived at their new homes.

9. Look at Number 9 at the top of the column. Inside a wagon you would probably find a—*cow ... barrel of water ... saddle ... chair.* Mark the space beside your answer.

10. This paragraph mainly tells about a—*pioneer family ... wagon train ... covered wagon ... long journey.*

11. The story says a covered wagon—*moved quickly in good weather ... carried just one person ... allowed people to travel comfortably ... was easy to build.* Mark the space beside your answer.

12. Look at Number 12. What might be found on the outside of a wagon? Is it—*a small table ... dress-up clothes ... a sack of canned food ... the family's dishes?*

It's time to stop working. You have finished lesson 8a.

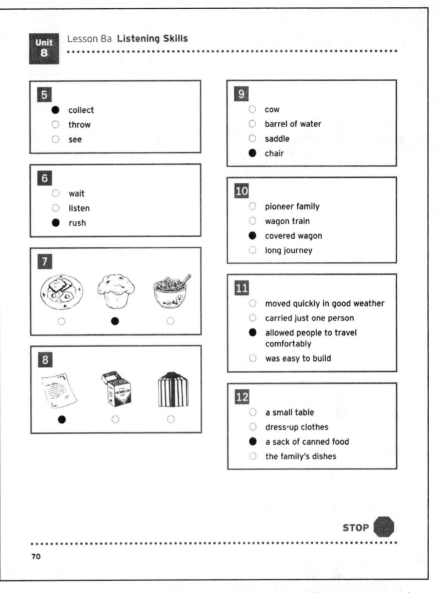

Review the answers with the students. Discuss why it is so important for the students to listen carefully while they look at the answer choices, mark the answer they think is correct, and then get ready for the next item.

Have the students indicate completion of the lesson by entering their score for this activity on the progress chart at the beginning of the book. Provide the students whatever help is necessary to record their scores.

Focus

Listening Skills
- identifying synonyms for orally presented words in context
- choosing a picture to answer questions about an orally presented story
- answering questions about an orally presented story

Test-taking Skills
- following oral directions
- listening carefully
- understanding unusual item formats
- staying with the first answer
- choosing a picture to answer questions
- taking the best guess when unsure of the answer

Samples A, B, and C

Say Turn to Lesson 8b on page 71. The page number is at the bottom of the page on the right.

Check to see that the students have found the right page.

Say In this lesson, you will answer more questions about sentences or stories I read to you. Find Sample A at the top of the page. I will read a sentence. The last part of the sentence will be missing. Then I will read the three answers for the item. You should choose the word that means the same as the word from the sentence. Mr. Howard *split* the watermelon among the children. To *split* is to—*divide into pieces ... plant ... eat quickly.* Which word means the same as *split?* *(pause)* The correct answer is *divide into pieces.* Mark the first answer space. Be sure your answer is filled in with a dark mark.

Check to see that the students have filled in the correct space.

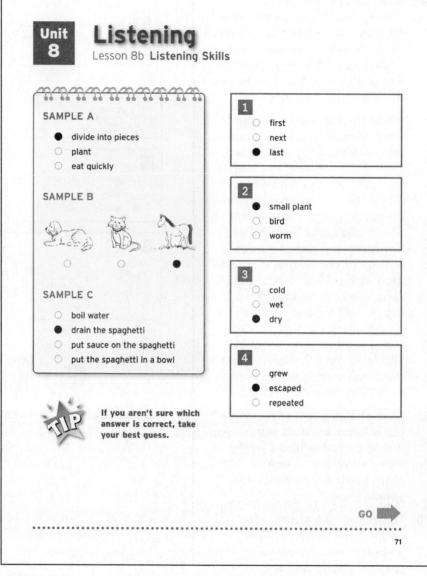

Unit 8 **Listening**
Lesson 8b **Listening Skills**

Say Now we'll do Sample B. Look at the three pictures and listen to this story.

The children in school were talking about their pets. Sona had a horse, John had a cat, and Ila had a dog.

Which picture shows Sona's pet? Is it a— *dog ... cat ...* or was it *a horse? (pause)* Sona's pet is *a horse.* Mark the last answer space. Press your pencil firmly so your mark comes out dark.

Check to see that the students have marked the correct space.

Say Look at Sample C. I will read a story and ask you a question about it. I will also read the answer choices that are written in your book. Listen carefully.

Lance helped his mother prepare dinner. First they made the sauce for the spaghetti. Then they boiled water. Lance's mother put the spaghetti into the water. When it was finished, she drained the spaghetti and put it in a big bowl. With his mother's help, Lance poured the sauce on the spaghetti.

What did Lance's mother do right after the spaghetti had cooked? Did she—*boil water … drain the spaghetti … put sauce on the spaghetti … put the spaghetti in a bowl?* Which answer is correct? *(pause)* The second answer is correct. Lance's mother cooked the spaghetti and then drained the spaghetti. Mark the space beside the second answer. Press your pencil firmly so your mark comes out dark.

Check to see that the students have marked the correct space.

TIP

Say Now let's look at the tip.

Read the tip aloud to the students.

Say It is important that you listen carefully to what I say and look at the words or pictures. As soon as you know which answer is correct, mark your answer and get ready for the next item. Don't change your answer unless you are sure it is wrong and another answer is better. When you are not sure which answer is correct, take your best guess.

Practice

Say Now you will do more items. Listen carefully to what I say as you look at the answer choices. Fill in your answer spaces with dark marks and completely erase any marks for answers that you change. Do you have any questions? Let's begin.

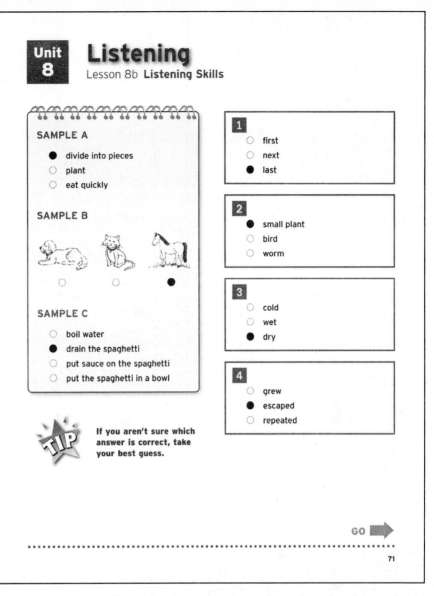

71

Pause between items to allow time for the students to fill in their answers.

1. Look at the first group of words. This is the *final* page of the book. *Final* means—*first … next … last.* Which word means the same as *final?* Mark the space for your answer.

2. The first *sprout* appeared in the garden. A sprout is a—*small plant … bird … worm.*

3. We had a *drought* last summer. During a *drought,* it is very—*cold … wet … dry.*

4. Move down to Number 4. Jennie's bird *got away. Got away* means the same as—*grew … escaped … repeated.*

   Turn to the next page, page 72.

Check to see that the students have found the right page. Allow time for students to relax.

Say Now we will do a different kind of activity. I will read some stories and ask you questions about them. You will choose the picture that is the best answer to each question.

Look at the pictures for Number 5 and listen to this story. Deanna got the mayonnaise out of the refrigerator. Then she took the lid off.

5. Which picture shows how the jar looked after Deanna took the lid off? Mark the space for your answer.

Here is another story. There will be two questions about it. Zenia was outside playing on the lawn. She was trying to stand on her head. Her friend, Letitia, could do this trick. Finally, after many tries, she succeeded. She shouted, "Look at me!" to her brother who was riding by in his toy car. He stopped and clapped for her. They made so much noise that Zenia's older sister and other brother stopped what they were doing and came to the window.

6. Move down to Number 6. What did Zenia succeed at doing? Was it—*jumping far … balancing on one foot …* or *standing on her head*? Mark the space for your answer.

7. To whom did Zenia shout, "Look at me!" Mark the space under your answer.

Here is another story. There will be one question about it. Dan wrote a letter to his grandmother. He put it in an envelope and wrote her address on the envelope. He sealed the envelope, then he started walking toward the door. "Did you forget something?" his mother asked?

8. Look at Number 8. What did Dan forget? Was it—*a gift … a pen …* or *a stamp*?

Look at the answers in the next column.

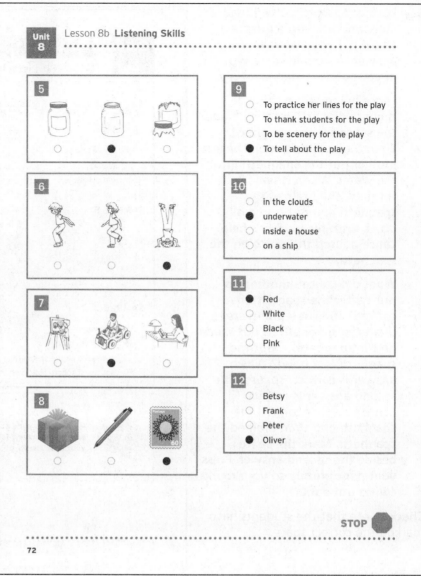

Unit 8 Lesson 8b **Listening Skills**

9.
- ○ To practice her lines for the play
- ○ To thank students for the play
- ○ To be scenery for the play
- ● To tell about the play

10.
- ○ in the clouds
- ● underwater
- ○ inside a house
- ○ on a ship

11.
- ● Red
- ○ White
- ○ Black
- ○ Pink

12.
- ○ Betsy
- ○ Frank
- ○ Peter
- ● Oliver

STOP

72

Say Now we will do another activity. I will read a story and ask you four questions about it. I will read the answers aloud while you read along silently. You will choose the answer you think is right. Let's begin.

Zoe's class was putting on a play for the rest of the school. For weeks, the students practiced their lines. They all made fins and fish masks out of cardboard for their costumes. The whole class helped paint blue waves and seaweed for the scenery. Then Zoe decided to make a poster to hang in the office to let students and parents know about the play. Her teacher brought her a big sheet of white paper, but Zoe wasn't sure where to start. Her friend Peter brought some paints and helped her write on the poster. Then Oliver used his glue and glitter to make the poster sparkle. Next, Betsy attached long ribbons of red paper to the sides of the poster. The ribbons fluttered whenever someone walked by. Last, Frank blew up some balloons and tied them to the corners of the poster. Zoe and her friends stood back to look at the poster. It was wonderful. Everyone in the school would notice it!

9. Why did Zoe make the poster? Was it—
To practice her lines for the play … To thank students for the play … To be scenery for the play … or To tell about the play? Mark your answer.

10. You can tell that Zoe's play takes place—
in the clouds … underwater … inside a house … on a ship.

11. What color was the paper Betsy put on the poster? Was it—*Red … White … Black … or Pink?*

12. Look at Number 12. Who was the second person to help Zoe with the poster? Was it—*Betsy … Frank … Peter … or Oliver?*

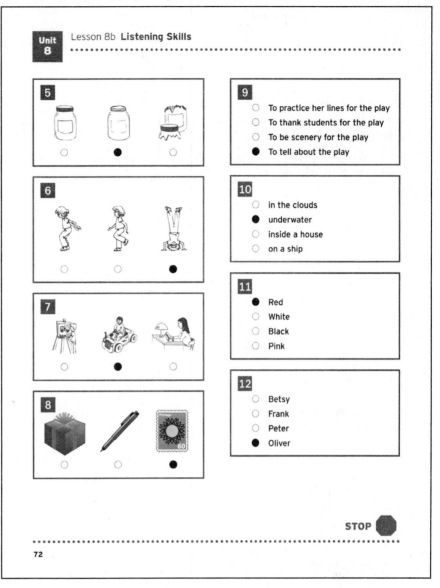

5

6

7

8

9
○ To practice her lines for the play
○ To thank students for the play
○ To be scenery for the play
● To tell about the play

10
○ in the clouds
● underwater
○ inside a house
○ on a ship

11
● Red
○ White
○ Black
○ Pink

12
○ Betsy
○ Frank
○ Peter
● Oliver

STOP

72

It's time to stop working. You have finished lesson 8b.

Review the answers with the students. Read the stories and have volunteers give the answers.

Have the students indicate completion of the lesson by entering their score for this activity on the progress chart at the beginning of the book. Provide the students whatever help is necessary to record their scores.

Focus

Listening Skills
- identifying synonyms for orally presented words in context
- choosing a picture to answer questions about an orally presented story
- answering questions about an orally presented story

Test-taking Skills
- following oral directions
- listening carefully
- understanding unusual item formats
- marking the right answer as soon as it is found
- choosing a picture to answer a question
- staying with the first answer
- taking the best guess when unsure of the answer

This lesson simulates an actual test-taking experience. Therefore, it is recommended that the directions be read verbatim and the suggested procedures be followed.

Unit 8 Test Yourself: Listening

SAMPLE A
- ○ rest
- ● prize
- ○ drink

SAMPLE B
- ○ cross it
- ○ find it
- ● make it

1
- ● shout
- ○ jump
- ○ stand

2
- ○ dirty
- ● cracked
- ○ missing

3
- ○ interesting
- ○ friendly
- ● quiet

4
- ○ keep
- ● share
- ○ pass

5
- ○ wash
- ○ paint
- ● cut

6
- ○ funny
- ○ helpful
- ● surprising

GO ➡

73

Directions

Administration Time: approximately 35 minutes

Say Turn to the Test Yourself lesson on page 73.

Check to be sure the students have found the right page. Point out to the students that this Test Yourself lesson is like a real test, but that they will score it themselves to see how well they are doing. Explain that it is important to answer as many questions as possible. Remind the students to listen carefully and to take the best guess when they are unsure of the answer.

Say This lesson will check how well you remember the listening skills you practiced in other lessons. Be sure your answer spaces are completely filled in. Press your pencil firmly so that your marks come out dark. Completely erase any marks for answers that you change. Do not write anything except your answers in your book. Find Sample A at the top of the page. I will read a sentence. The last part of the sentence will be missing. Then I will read the three answers for the item. You should choose the answer that best completes the sentence. Listen carefully.

The person who finishes the race first will get an *award*. An *award* is a—*rest ... prize ... drink*. Mark your answer.

Allow time for the students to fill in their answers.

Say The second answer is correct. If you chose another answer, erase yours and fill in the space beside *prize* now.

Check to see that the students have marked the correct space.

Say Now we'll do another kind of activity. Look at the answers for Sample B and listen carefully. We learned how to *build* a bridge out of old logs. To *build* a bridge means to—*cross it … find it … make it.* Mark the space for your answer.

Allow time for the students to fill in their answers.

Say To *build* a bridge means to *make it,* so you should have filled in the last answer space. If you chose another answer, erase yours and fill in the last answer space now.

Check to see that the students have marked the correct space.

Say Now we will do more items like the samples. Listen to what I say and look at the answers in your book. Mark the space for your answer.

Pause between items to allow time for students to fill in their answers.

1. Look at the first group of words. The crowd always cheers when we shoot a basket. To *cheer* means to—*shout … jump … stand.*

2. She put the *broken* dish in the garbage can. Broken means the same as—*dirty … cracked … missing.*

3. Move over to Number 3. The garden was a *peaceful* place to be. *Peaceful* means the same as—*interesting … friendly … quiet.*

4. I *split* my sandwich with Sam. To *split* means to—*keep … share … pass.*

5. We sometimes *clip* our dog's toenails. To *clip* means to—*wash … paint … cut.*

6. Move down to Number 6. It was *amazing* when my little brother sang the alphabet song by himself. Something that is *amazing* is—*funny … helpful … surprising.*

   Turn to the next page, page 74.

Check to see that the students have found the right page. Allow time for students to relax.

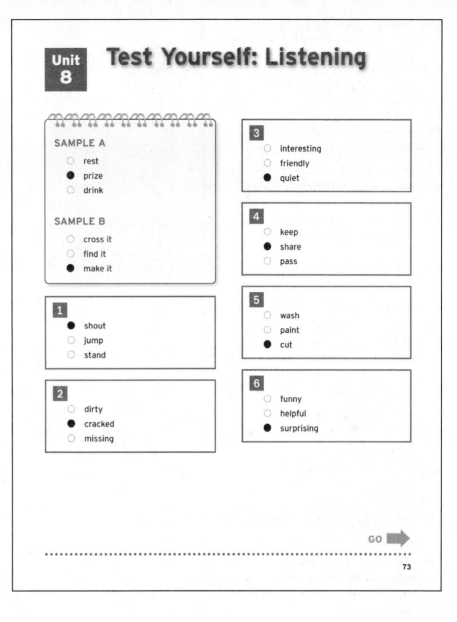

Say Now we'll do something different. I will read a story and you will answer two questions about it. Look at the three pictures for Sample C and listen to this story.

Be sure the students have found Sample C.

Say A turtle carries its home on its back. When danger approaches, the turtle pulls its head and legs into its shell. Other water animals, like snakes or fish, use speed to escape enemies. Turtles, however, just wait for the danger to go away. Another animal, the hermit crab, also carries a shell around with it. Unlike the turtle, the hermit crab borrows the old shell of another animal.

Look at Sample C. Which water animal does <u>not</u> use speed to escape from enemies? Is it *a snake … a fish …* or *a turtle?* Mark your answer.

Allow time for the students to fill in their answers.

Say *A turtle* does not use speed to escape its enemies, so you should have filled in the last answer space. If you chose another answer, erase yours and fill in the last answer space now.

Check to see that the students have marked the correct space.

Say Move down to Sample D. Which animal borrows a shell for its home? Is it a—*clam … hermit crab …* or *snail?* Mark your answer.

Allow time for the students to fill in their answers.

Say *A hermit crab* borrows a shell for its home, so you should have filled in the second answer space. If you chose another answer, erase yours and fill in the second answer space now.

Check to see that the students have marked the correct space.

74

Say Now we will do more items like Samples C and D. Listen to what I say and look at the answers in your book. Mark the space for your answer.

Pause between items to allow time for students to fill in their answers.

Say Paul was sitting under a tree. He had come to the park with his dog, Mollie. She was a medium-sized dog with long hair and a bushy tail. Mollie was standing beside Paul with her tail wagging. This meant she wanted to play. Paul stood up and threw a plastic disk. Mollie ran after it, jumped into the air, and caught it. She ran back to Paul and sat down with the disk in her mouth. Paul knew Mollie wanted to play some more, but it was time to go home. Paul got on his bike and rode slowly across the park. Mollie could keep up with him because he rode slowly. When they reached the end of the park, Paul saw his friend, Sam, with his dog, Sandy. Sam was hooking a leash to Sandy's collar. Paul got off his bike and hooked Molly's leash on her collar. It was a smart thing to do before they all crossed the street.

7. Look at Row 7 under the samples. At the beginning of the story, what was Paul sitting near? Was it—*a bench ... a tree ... a fountain?*

8. What did Mollie probably look like? Mark under your answer.

9. Move over to the top of next column. What did Paul throw to Mollie? Was it—*a ball ... a stick ... or a plastic disk?*

10. How did Paul get home? Did he use—*a bike ... a scooter ... or in-line skates?*

11. Look at Number 11. What did Sam do at the end of the park? Did he—*brush Sandy ... put a leash on Sandy ... wait for his mother?*

   Turn to the next page, page 75.

Check to see that the students have found the right page. Allow time for students to relax.

Say Look at Samples E and F at the top of the page. I will read a story and ask you two questions about it.

Check to be sure the students have found the samples.

Say Sonny's baby brother was crying. Sonny knew just what to do. He stepped outside and pressed his face against the sliding glass door. Sonny made one silly face after another. Pretty soon the baby stopped crying and started giggling. When Mom returned to the room, she was pleased Sonny had made the baby happy, but she was not pleased with the face marks all over the glass. Before Sonny knew it, he was washing the glass door.

Look at the answers for Sample E and listen carefully. Why did Sonny probably wash the glass door? *It had fingerprints on it. … His mom asked him to. … He wanted to make money. … It made the baby giggle.* Mark your answer.

Allow time for the students to fill in their answers.

Say The second answer is correct. *His mom asked him to.* You should have filled in the second answer space. If you chose another answer, erase yours and fill in the second answer space now.

Check to see that the students have marked the correct space.

Say Look at the answers for Sample F. What did Sonny do to get his brother to laugh? *Made faces … Told jokes … Did a dance … Went and hid.* Mark the space for your answer.

Allow time for the students to fill in their answers.

Say The first answer, *Made faces,* is correct. If you chose another answer, erase yours and fill in the first answer space now.

Check to see that the students have marked the correct space.

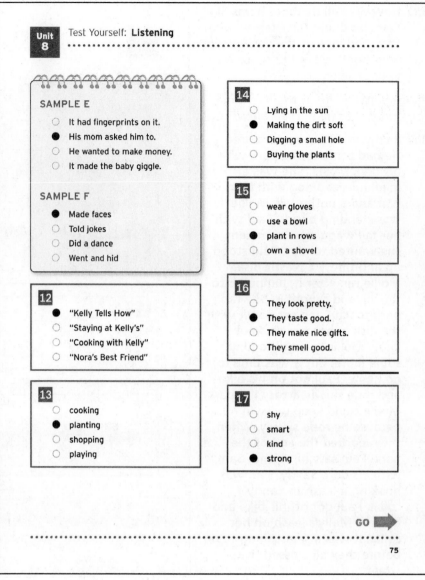

Unit 8 — Test Yourself: **Listening**

SAMPLE E
- ○ It had fingerprints on it.
- ● His mom asked him to.
- ○ He wanted to make money.
- ○ It made the baby giggle.

SAMPLE F
- ● Made faces
- ○ Told jokes
- ○ Did a dance
- ○ Went and hid

12
- ● "Kelly Tells How"
- ○ "Staying at Kelly's"
- ○ "Cooking with Kelly"
- ○ "Nora's Best Friend"

13
- ○ cooking
- ● planting
- ○ shopping
- ○ playing

14
- ○ Lying in the sun
- ● Making the dirt soft
- ○ Digging a small hole
- ○ Buying the plants

15
- ○ wear gloves
- ○ use a bowl
- ● plant in rows
- ○ own a shovel

16
- ○ They look pretty.
- ● They taste good.
- ○ They make nice gifts.
- ○ They smell good.

17
- ○ shy
- ○ smart
- ○ kind
- ● strong

GO ➡

75

Say Now we will do more items like Samples E and F. Listen to what I say and look at the answers in your book. Mark the space for your answer.

Pause between items to allow time for students to fill in their answers.

Say Listen to Kelly tell her friend, Nora, how to do something. "You should try it. First, choose a sunny spot in your yard. Strawberries need a lot of sun. Then get the dirt ready. You will need a shovel and a hose. Use the shovel to break up the dirt and the hose to get it wet. When the dirt is ready, dig a small hole, a couple of inches down. Put the bottom part of the plant in the hole and fill it up with dirt again. Now you are ready to dig another hole. If you plant in rows, you can pick the fruit more easily later. And when you taste your first strawberry, you will know why I like growing them!"

12. Look at Number 12. What is a good name for this story? Is it— *"Kelly Tells How" ... "Staying at Kelly's" ... "Cooking with Kelly" ... or "Nora's Best Friend"?*

13. Are these directions for— *cooking ... planting ... shopping ... or playing?*

14. What comes right after choosing a sunny spot? *Lying in the sun ... Making the dirt soft ... Digging a small hole ... or Buying the plants?*

15. Kelly says picking strawberries is easier when you—*wear gloves ... use a bowl ... plant in rows ... own a shovel.*

16. Move down to Number 16. Why does Kelly like growing strawberries? Is it because—*They look pretty. ... They taste good. ... They make nice gifts. ... or They smell good?*

Here is another story. The first question about the story is on this page. The rest of the questions are on the next page.

On Tuesday Mrs. Tubman said a new girl would be joining the class. Mrs. Tubman said the girl would need a buddy, someone to help show her around. Melissa had been a new

---

SAMPLE E
- ○ It had fingerprints on it.
- ● His mom asked him to.
- ○ He wanted to make money.
- ○ It made the baby giggle.

SAMPLE F
- ● Made faces
- ○ Told jokes
- ○ Did a dance
- ○ Went and hid

12
- ● "Kelly Tells How"
- ○ "Staying at Kelly's"
- ○ "Cooking with Kelly"
- ○ "Nora's Best Friend"

13
- ○ cooking
- ● planting
- ○ shopping
- ○ playing

14
- ○ Lying in the sun
- ● Making the dirt soft
- ○ Digging a small hole
- ○ Buying the plants

15
- ○ wear gloves
- ○ use a bowl
- ● plant in rows
- ○ own a shovel

16
- ○ They look pretty.
- ● They taste good.
- ○ They make nice gifts.
- ○ They smell good.

17
- ○ shy
- ○ smart
- ○ kind
- ● strong

GO ➡

75

---

student once, and she remembered how hard it had been to find her way around. She wanted to be the new girl's buddy, but she waited to see if anyone else was interested. Mrs. Tubman smiled when Melissa finally raised her hand. When the new girl showed up, the teacher introduced Melissa. "Your buddy Melissa is a very bright student. Why, she even won the spelling bee last month!" Melissa's face turned bright pink, but Mrs. Tubman's words made her feel good. Melissa smiled at the new girl and led her to the desk beside her own.

17. All of these words can be used to describe Melissa except—*shy ... smart ... kind ... strong.*

Turn to the next page, page 76.

Check to see that the students have found the right page. Allow time for students to relax.

Say Look at Number 18 at the top of the first column. What did Melissa do right before she raised her hand? She—*watched her classmates ... asked a question ... checked the spelling ... turned bright pink.*

19. What made Melissa feel good at the end of the story? *She sat at the teacher's desk. ... She got to leave the classroom. ... The new girl was friendly. ... The teacher said nice things.*

    Kevin Lowell spent all of one Sunday afternoon making bread with his grandmother. His grandma mixed together the yeast, sugar, and water, and Kevin measured the flour. Grandma helped Kevin stir and knead the mound of sticky dough. While the dough was rising, they went to sit on Grandma's front porch. After an hour, Grandma shaped the dough into loaves. She said that Kevin should check the bread in half an hour. If it had risen above the edge of the pans, Kevin could put the loaves in the oven to bake.

20. Kevin can best be described as—*helpful ... careful ... whiny ... proud.*

21. What will Kevin probably do pretty soon? *Knead the bread ... Clean the kitchen ... Make some cookies ... Bake the bread.*

22. A good title for this story would be—*"Summer Sundays" ... "A Fine Family Dinner" ... "Baking and Being Together" ... "Too Many Cooks in the Kitchen."*

23. Look at Number 23. What did Kevin do while Grandma mixed together the yeast, sugar, and water? *Measured the flour ... Got out the loaf pans ... Turned on the oven ... The paragraph does not say.*

24. You can tell from the paragraph that Grandma is—*impatient with people ... an experienced baker ... rarely around Kevin ... a professional cook.*

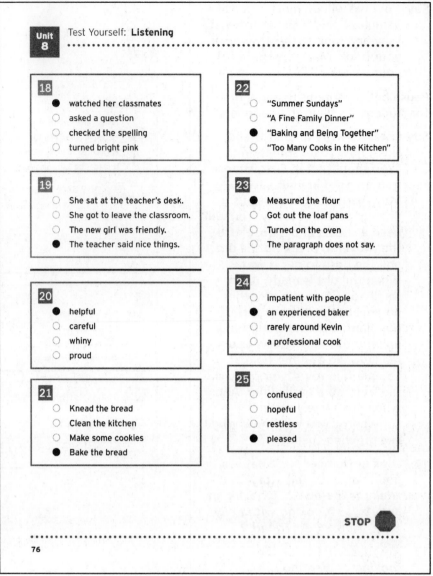

Unit 8 — Test Yourself: **Listening**

18.
● watched her classmates
○ asked a question
○ checked the spelling
○ turned bright pink

19.
○ She sat at the teacher's desk.
○ She got to leave the classroom.
○ The new girl was friendly.
● The teacher said nice things.

20.
● helpful
○ careful
○ whiny
○ proud

21.
○ Knead the bread
○ Clean the kitchen
○ Make some cookies
● Bake the bread

22.
○ "Summer Sundays"
○ "A Fine Family Dinner"
● "Baking and Being Together"
○ "Too Many Cooks in the Kitchen"

23.
● Measured the flour
○ Got out the loaf pans
○ Turned on the oven
○ The paragraph does not say.

24.
○ impatient with people
● an experienced baker
○ rarely around Kevin
○ a professional cook

25.
○ confused
○ hopeful
○ restless
● pleased

STOP

76

25. Look at Number 25. At the end of the story, Kevin and his grandma probably felt—*confused ... hopeful ... restless ... pleased.*

    It's time to stop. You have completed the Test Yourself lesson.

Review the answers with the students. Have the students indicate completion of the lesson by entering their score for this activity on the progress chart at the beginning of the book. Provide the students whatever help is necessary to record their scores.

Test Practice

To the Teacher:

The Test Practice unit provides the students with an opportunity to apply the reading, mathematics, spelling, language, listening, and test-taking skills practiced in the lessons of this book. It is also a final practice activity to be used prior to administering the Stanford Achievement Test. By following the step-by-step instructions on the subsequent pages, you will be able to simulate the structured atmosphere in which achievement tests are given. Take time to become familiar with the administrative procedures before the students take the tests.

Scheduling the Tests

Each test should be administered in a separate session. Two sessions may be scheduled for the same day if a sufficient break in time is provided between sessions.

Test	Administration Time (minutes)
1 Word Study Skills	20
2 Reading Vocabulary	25
3 Reading Comprehension	60
4 Mathematics Problem Solving	60
5 Mathematics Procedures	25
6 Spelling	15
7 Language	45
8 Listening	35

Preparing for the Tests

1. Put a "Testing—Do Not Disturb" sign on the classroom door to eliminate unnecessary interruptions.

2. Make sure the students are seated at a comfortable distance from each other and that their desks are clear.

3. Provide each student with sharpened pencils with erasers. Have an extra supply of pencils available. For the mathematics tests, provide each student with scratch paper.

4. Distribute the students' books.

5. Encourage the students with a "pep talk."

Administering the Tests

1. Read the "Say" copy verbatim to the students and follow all the instructions that are given.

2. Make sure the students understand the directions for each test before proceeding.

3. Move about the classroom during testing to see that the students are following the directions. Make sure the students are working on the correct page and are marking their answers properly.

4. Without distracting the students, provide test-taking tips at your discretion.

Test 1
Word Study Skills

Administration Time: *20 minutes*

Say The final part of *Scoring High* is called Test Practice. It will give you a chance to practice all the reading, mathematics, spelling, language, and listening skills you learned in other lessons. The first section of the Test Practice is called Test 1 Word Study Skills. Turn to page 77 of your book.

Check to see that the students have found page 77.

Say Find Sample A in the box near the top of the page. Read the words to yourself as I read them aloud—*rewrite … fallen … popcorn.* Which of the words has two smaller words in it? Mark the space for your answer.

Allow time for the students to fill in their answers.

Say You should have filled in the third answer, *popcorn.* If you chose another answer, erase yours and fill in the third answer now.

Check to see that the students have marked the correct space.

Say Now you will do some more items just as you did Sample A. For Numbers 1 through 4, read the three words. Fill in the space under the word that has two words in it. Only do Numbers 1 through 4. You will do the other items later. Fill in your answer spaces with dark marks and completely erase any marks for answers that you change. Do you have any questions? Start working now.

Allow enough time for the students to do Numbers 1 through 4.

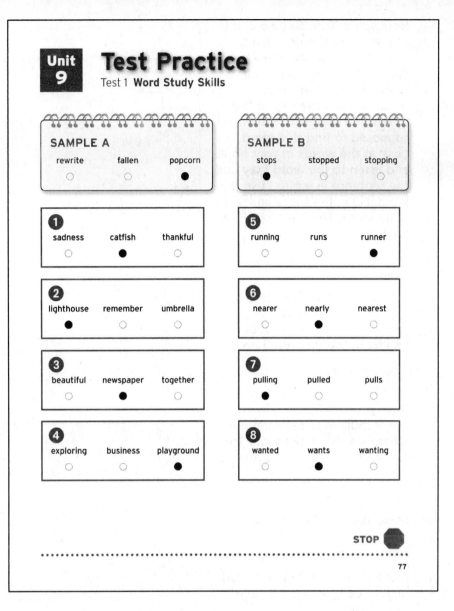

Say Now you will do Sample B. It is at the top of the right-hand column. Look at the three words. They are almost the same but have different endings. I will use one of the words in a sentence. You are supposed to find that word. Look at the words in your book and listen to the word I say and the sentence in which I use the word. Fill in the space under the word *stops*. The bus *stops* here. *Stops*.

Allow time for the students to fill in their answers.

Say You should have filled in the first answer. If you chose another answer, erase yours and fill in the first space now.

Check to see that the students have marked the correct space.

Say Now you will do more items like Sample B. Listen carefully to what I say. Fill in the space for the answer you think is correct.

Allow time between items for the students to fill in their answers.

5. Move down to Number 5. *Runner*. Maria's mother is a *runner. Runner.*

6. Move down to Number 6. Mark under *nearly*. It is *nearly* lunch time. *Nearly.*

7. Move down to Number 7. Mark beside *pulling*. The horse was *pulling* a wagon. *Pulling.*

8. Go to the last row. *Wants*. Harry *wants* a new bike. *Wants.*

Allow a moment for the students to relax.

Say Look at the next page, page 78.

Check to be sure the students have found the correct page.

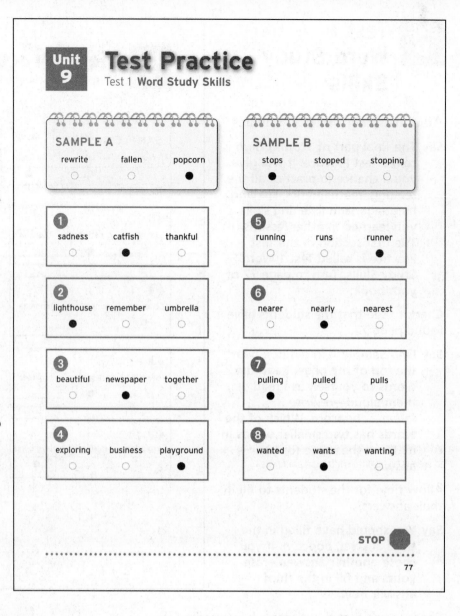

Say Now you will do Sample C. It is in the box at the top of the page. The three words are *can't … don't … won't*. These words are shortened forms of other words. I will say two words and then use them in a sentence. Listen carefully. *Do not.* Our neighbors *do not* have a pet. Fill in the space under the word that means the same as *do not*.

Allow time for the students to fill in their answers.

Say The second answer is correct. If you chose another answer, erase yours and fill in the space under the second answer now.

Check to see that the students have marked the correct space.

Say Now you will do more items like Sample C. Listen carefully to what I say. Fill in the space for the answer you think is correct.

Allow time between items for the students to fill in their answers.

9. Put your finger on Number 9 under Sample C. Which answer means *there is? There is* Jenny. *There is.*

10. Move down to Number 10. Which word means *he is? He is* coming to the game. *He is.*

11. Go to Number 11. Which answer means *they are? They are* in my class. *They are.*

12. Go down to Number 12. Which answer means *we will?* Tomorrow *we will* go to the movies. *We will.*

Allow a moment for the students to relax.

Say Find Sample D in the next column of the page. The first word you see is *page.* The letter *g* in *page* has a line under it. Now look at the other three words in the box. Mark the space under the word that has the same /j/ sound as *page.*

Allow time for the students to fill in their answers.

Say The second answer, *jump,* is correct. If you chose another answer, erase yours and fill in the space under *jump* now.

Check to see that the students have correctly filled in their answer spaces with a dark mark.

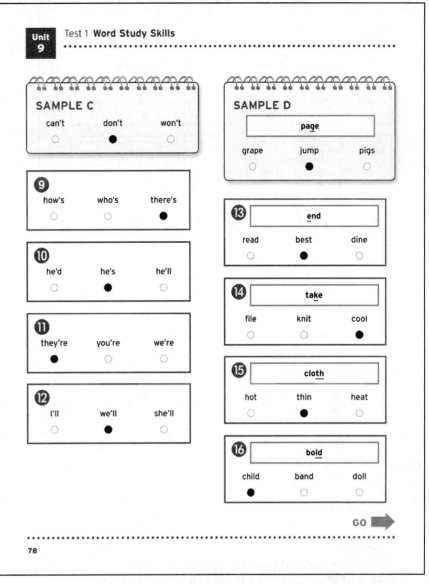

Say Now you will do more items just as you did Sample D. Say the word with the underlined part to yourself. Think about the sound made by the underlined part. Then look at the answer choices. Fill in the space under the answer that has the same sound as the underlined part of the first word. If you are not sure which answer is correct, take your best guess. Fill in your answer spaces with dark marks. When you see a GO sign at the bottom of the page, turn the page and continue working. Work until you come to the STOP sign at the bottom of page 80. Completely erase any marks for answers that you change. Do you have any questions? Start working now.

Allow time for the students to fill in their answers.

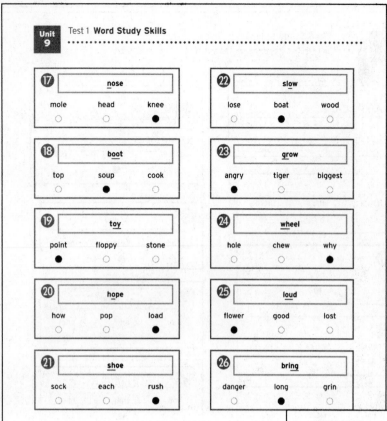

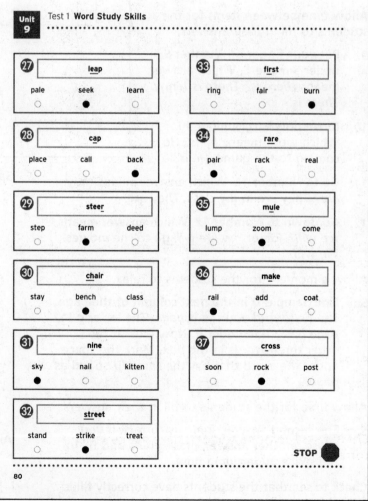

Say It's time to stop. You have finished Test 1. Check to see that you have completely filled in your answer circles with dark marks. Make sure that any marks for answers that you changed have been completely erased. Now you may close your book.

Review the items with the students. Have them indicate completion of the lesson by entering their score for this activity on the progress chart at the beginning of the book. Provide the students whatever help is necessary to record their scores. Then collect the students' books if this is the end of the testing session.

Test 2
Reading Vocabulary

Administration Time: 25 minutes

Say Turn to page 81 of your book. This is Test 2 Reading Vocabulary.

Check to see that the students have found page 81.

Say This lesson will check how well you remember the vocabulary skills you practiced in other lessons. Be sure your answer spaces are completely filled in. Press your pencil firmly so your marks come out dark. Completely erase any marks for answers that you change. Do not write anything except your answers in your book.

Find Sample A in the box at the top of the page. Read Sample A to yourself as I read it aloud. *A feast is a kind of—party … fight … meal … animal.* Which of the four answers means about the same as the underlined word? Mark the space for your answer.

Allow time for the students to fill in their answers.

Say You should have filled in the third answer, *meal.* If you chose another answer, erase yours and fill in the space beside *meal* now.

Check to see that the students have marked the correct space.

Say Now do Sample B yourself. Which of the four answers means about the same as the underlined word? Mark the space for your answer.

Allow time for the students to fill in their answers.

Say You should have filled in the third answer, *say.* If you chose another answer, erase yours and fill in the space beside *say* now.

Check to see that the students have marked the correct space.

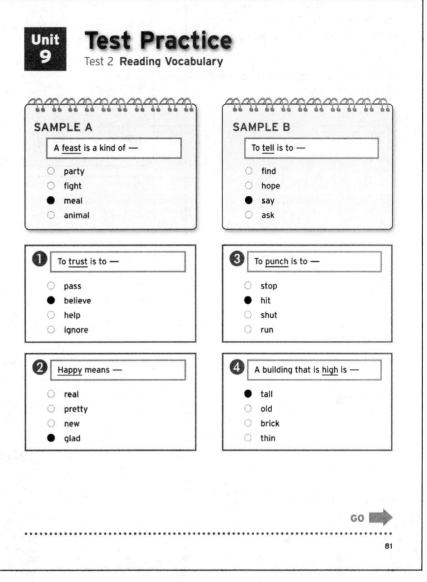

Say Now you will do some more items. Complete the items on this page. When you come to the GO sign at the bottom of the page, go on to the next page and continue working. Work until you come to the STOP sign at the bottom of page 82. Fill in your answer spaces with dark marks and completely erase any marks for answers that you change. Do you have any questions? Start working now.

Allow time for the students to fill in their answers.

Say It's time to stop. You have finished the first part of the lesson. Turn to the next page, page 83.

Check to see that the students have found the right page.

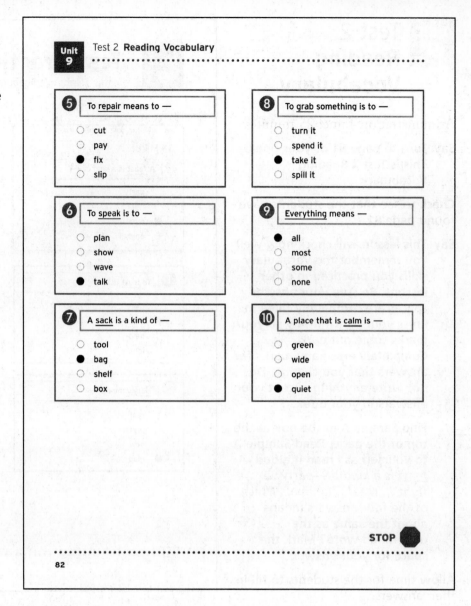

Unit 9   Test 2 **Reading Vocabulary**

5 To <u>repair</u> means to —
- ○ cut
- ○ pay
- ● fix
- ○ slip

6 To <u>speak</u> is to —
- ○ plan
- ○ show
- ○ wave
- ● talk

7 A <u>sack</u> is a kind of —
- ○ tool
- ● bag
- ○ shelf
- ○ box

8 To <u>grab</u> something is to —
- ○ turn it
- ○ spend it
- ● take it
- ○ spill it

9 <u>Everything</u> means —
- ● all
- ○ most
- ○ some
- ○ none

10 A place that is <u>calm</u> is —
- ○ green
- ○ wide
- ○ open
- ● quiet

STOP

82

Say In this part of the Test Practice you will use the meaning of a sentence to identify words. Read the sentence for Sample C to yourself while I read it aloud. *Try not to <u>miss</u> the basket.* In which sentence does the word *miss* mean the same thing as in the sentence above? The answers are: *Did you <u>miss</u> me yesterday? ... Don't <u>miss</u> this movie. ... He might <u>miss</u> the target. ... I <u>miss</u> my cousins in Texas.* Mark the space for your answer.

Allow time for the students to fill in their answers.

Say You should have filled in the third answer space. If you chose another answer, erase yours and fill in the third answer space now.

Check to see that the students have marked the correct space.

Say Now you will do some more items. Complete the items on this page just as we did Sample C. Work until you come to the STOP sign at the bottom of the page. Fill in your answer spaces with dark marks and completely erase any marks for answers that you change. Do you have any questions? Start working now.

Allow time for the students to fill in their answers.

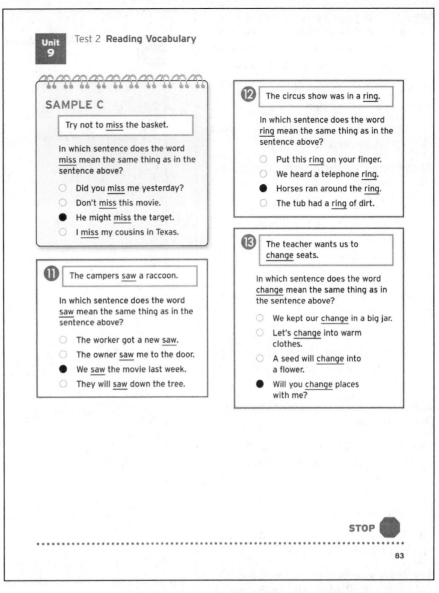

SAMPLE C

Try not to <u>miss</u> the basket.

In which sentence does the word <u>miss</u> mean the same thing as in the sentence above?

○ Did you <u>miss</u> me yesterday?
○ Don't <u>miss</u> this movie.
● He might <u>miss</u> the target.
○ I <u>miss</u> my cousins in Texas.

11 The campers <u>saw</u> a raccoon.

In which sentence does the word <u>saw</u> mean the same thing as in the sentence above?

○ The worker got a new <u>saw</u>.
○ The owner <u>saw</u> me to the door.
● We <u>saw</u> the movie last week.
○ They will <u>saw</u> down the tree.

12 The circus show was in a <u>ring</u>.

In which sentence does the word <u>ring</u> mean the same thing as in the sentence above?

○ Put this <u>ring</u> on your finger.
○ We heard a telephone <u>ring</u>.
● Horses ran around the <u>ring</u>.
○ The tub had a <u>ring</u> of dirt.

13 The teacher wants us to <u>change</u> seats.

In which sentence does the word <u>change</u> mean the same thing as in the sentence above?

○ We kept our <u>change</u> in a big jar.
○ Let's <u>change</u> into warm clothes.
○ A seed will <u>change</u> into a flower.
● Will you <u>change</u> places with me?

STOP

83

Say It's time to stop. You have finished this part of the lesson. Turn to the next page, page 84.

Check to see that the students have found the right page.

Say On this page, you will do a different kind of item. Look at Sample D. Read it to yourself as I read it aloud. *Those girls look similar because they are sisters. Similar means—smart … alike … small … tidy.* Which answer choice is correct? Mark the space for your answer.

Allow time for the students to fill in their answers.

Say You should have filled in the space for the second answer, *alike.* If you chose another answer, erase yours and fill in the second answer now.

Check to see that the students have marked the correct space.

Say Do Sample E yourself. Read the item carefully. Which answer is correct? Mark the space for your answer.

Allow time for the students to fill in their answers.

Say You should have filled in the first answer, *benches.* If you chose another answer, erase yours and fill in the space beside *benches* now.

Check to see that the students have marked the correct space.

Say Now you will do some more items. Complete the items on this page just as we did Samples D and E. Work until you come to the STOP sign at the bottom of the page. Fill in your answer spaces with dark marks and completely erase any marks for answers that you change. Do you have any questions? Start working now.

Allow time for the students to fill in their answers.

Say It's time to stop. You have finished Test 2. Check to see that you have completely filled in your answer circles with dark marks. Make sure that any marks for answers that you changed have been completely erased. Now you may close your book.

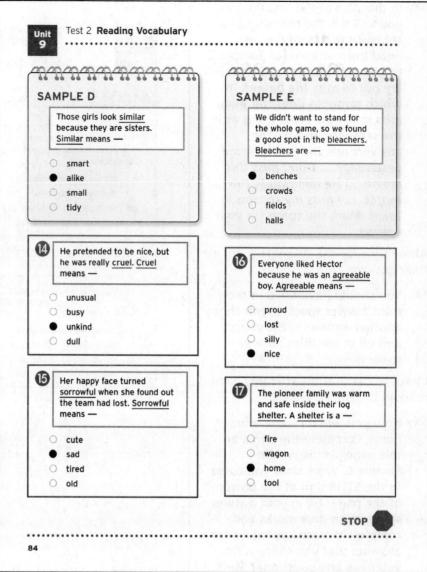

Review the items with the students. Have them indicate completion of the lesson by entering their score for this activity on the progress chart at the beginning of the book. Provide the students whatever help is necessary to record their scores. Then collect the students' books if this is the end of the testing session.

Administration Time: 60 minutes

Say Turn to the Test Practice section of your book on page 85. This is Test 3 Reading Comprehension.

Check to see that the students have found page 85.

Say This lesson will check how well you remember the comprehension skills you practiced in other lessons. Be sure your answer spaces are completely filled in. Press your pencil firmly so your marks come out dark. Completely erase any marks for answers that you change. Do not write anything except your answers in your book. Read the story for the samples to yourself and then read the question for Sample A. *Where does this story take place?* Mark the space for your answer.

Allow time for the students to fill in their answers.

Say You should have filled in the second answer, *On a street.* If you chose another answer, erase yours and fill in the second answer now.

Check to see that the students have marked the correct space.

Say Read the question for Sample B to yourself. Which answer is correct? You should look back at the story to find the answer. Mark the space for your answer.

Allow time for the students to fill in their answers.

Say You should have filled in the third answer. If you chose another answer, erase yours and fill in the space beside *A door opened* now.

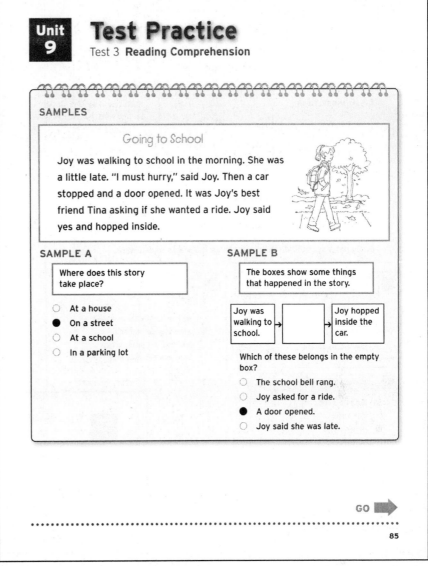

Check to see that the students have marked the correct space.

Say Now you will do some items by yourself. Look back at the stories to answer the questions. If you are not sure which answer is correct, take your best guess. When you see a GO sign at the bottom of a page, go on to the next page and continue working. Work until you come to the STOP sign at the bottom of page 92. Completely erase any marks for answers that you change. Do you have any questions? Start working now.

Allow time for the students to fill in their answers. Walk around the room and provide test-taking tips as necessary.

Park Rules

Help make our park a safe, clean place for everyone. We ask visitors to follow six simple rules:

1. Put all trash in garbage cans.

2. Keep pets on leashes.

3. Clean up after your pets.

4. Ride bikes only on the bike paths.

5. Children should be accompanied by an adult.

6. Do not leave food on the picnic tables. It attracts wild animals.

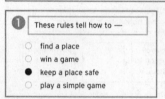

1 These rules tell how to —

○ find a place
○ win a game
● keep a place safe
○ play a simple game

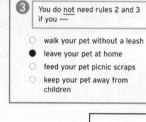

2 You will need rule 6 if you —

○ are with a child
○ ride a bike
● have a picnic
○ have a pet

3 You do not need rules 2 and 3 if you —

○ walk your pet without a leash
● leave your pet at home
○ feed your pet picnic scraps
○ keep your pet away from children

86

Earth Day

I like holidays. They are special days. Today is my favorite holiday. It is called Earth Day. It is a day to celebrate the Earth. People all over the world celebrate Earth Day. They do different things. They sing, dance, and hold parades. My family hikes on Earth Day. We pack a lunch and pick a trail. We hike all day. Everywhere we look we see the Earth's beauty. We celebrate the Earth's beauty on Earth Day.

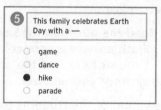

4 This story was written mainly to —

○ show how to do something
● tell what a family does on one day
○ get you to try something new
○ tell what a special place looks like

5 This family celebrates Earth Day with a —

○ game
○ dance
● hike
○ parade

GO ➡

87

Salad Pizza

"What is this?" asked Hannah. She pointed to a spinach plant in Grandma's garden.

"It goes in a salad," said Grandma.

"I love salad!" said Hannah.

"I know," said Grandma. "Let's pick some." Hannah and Grandma picked a little spinach. They put it in their basket.

"Are those for a salad, too?" asked Hannah. This time she pointed at some chives.

"Yes," said Grandma. "These are skinny onions. Smell them." Hannah put her face in the chives. She took a big sniff.

"Mmm," said Hannah. "They smell good."

Grandma and Hannah washed their basket of vegetables under the hose. After that, they went inside to make lunch.

Hannah stood on a short stool. Grandma rolled out a ball of white dough. Hanna was puzzled. What kind of salad had dough? Grandma put red tomato sauce on the dough. Then she chopped the spinach and the chives. She sprinkled them on top. Last, she added cheese. Grandma put the salad in the oven. Now Hannah was really surprised.

"Grandma?" asked Hannah. "Why are you baking our salad?"

Grandma wiped her hands on her apron and laughed. She could see why Hannah was confused.

"Our salad needs to be baked because it is part salad and part pizza," said Grandma.

6 In this story, the basket is for —

○ flowers
● vegetables
○ muffins
○ fruit

7 What did Hannah pick first?

● spinach
○ onions
○ tomatoes
○ lettuce

8 What will Grandma and Hannah probably do next?

○ put the pizza in the oven
○ go into the garden
● set the table for lunch
○ make a big green salad

9 The boxes show some things that happened in the story.

| Grandma rolled out the dough. | → | | → | Grandma chopped the spinach and chives. |

Which of these belongs in the empty box?

○ Grandma sprinkled cheese on.
● Grandma put tomato sauce on.
○ Grandma wiped her hands.
○ Grandma put it in the oven.

10 What did Hannah learn in this story?

○ Things that grow in gardens taste funny.
○ Making pizza dough is simple.
○ Caring for a garden is hard work.
● Things that go in salads go on pizzas, too.

GO ➡

The Missing Seeds

"Oh, dear, oh dear," said Squirrel. "Where did I put those seeds?"

He looked everywhere. They weren't in the tree trunk. They weren't under the stone. They weren't by the fence. <u>Where were they?</u>

"What are you looking for, Son?" Pappa asked.

"My sunflower seeds!" cried Squirrel. "I hid them here last month, but now I can't find them." Squirrel's eyes filled with tears. He thought Pappa would give him a scolding.

But Pappa wanted to help. "Try looking over there," he said. Pappa pointed to a patch of tall yellow flowers. They were the tallest flowers Squirrel had ever seen.

"I did not hide my seeds in a patch of flowers," said Squirrel. Still, he went to look. Suddenly, Squirrel's nose began to twitch. He smelled sunflower seeds. Then he started to dig.

11 Where did Squirrel look for the seeds?

- ○ In a hole
- ○ In a bush
- ○ In a nest
- ● In a tree

12 When Squirrel told Pappa what he was looking for, he felt —

- ○ angry
- ○ excited
- ● worried
- ○ hopeful

13 At the end of the story, Squirrel did not know that —

- ○ he could smell sunflower seeds
- ○ his Pappa wanted to help him
- ○ he hid the seeds a month ago
- ● his seeds had become flowers

14 What will probably happen next?

- ○ Pappa will get angry with Squirrel.
- ● Squirrel will keep looking for his seeds.
- ○ Pappa will go find his own seeds.
- ○ Squirrel will tell Pappa to go away.

GO ➡

Say It's time to stop. You have finished Test 3. Check to see that you have completely filled in your answer circles with dark marks. Make sure that any marks for answers that you changed have been completely erased. Now you may close your book.

Review the items with the students. Have them indicate completion of the lesson by entering their score for this activity on the progress chart at the beginning of the book. Provide the students whatever help is necessary to record their scores. Then collect the students' books if this is the end of the testing session.

Cheesy Noodles Contest
For Children Ages 5-10

How to Enter:

1. Buy a box of Cheesy Noodles.

2. Have a parent, grandparent, or other adult cook the Cheesy Noodles so you can taste them.

3. Write a song about Cheesy Noodles. Your song must be at least six lines long. It should tell why you like to eat Cheesy Noodles.

4. Send your song and the empty box of Cheesy Noodles to:

   Cheesy Noodles Company
   333 Tillamook Street
   Aberdeen, Wisconsin 53706

5. Be sure to send a stamped envelope with your name and address on it. We will send you information about the contest winners.

NOTE: Your song must be mailed <u>before</u> September 9. Winners will be flown by airplane to Wisconsin. They will get to be in a television ad for Cheesy Noodles. They will also win a free case of Cheesy Noodles.

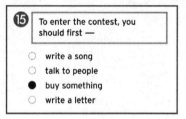

15 To enter the contest, you should first —

○ write a song
○ talk to people
● buy something
○ write a letter

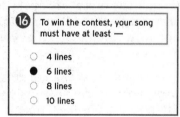

16 To win the contest, your song must have at least —

○ 4 lines
● 6 lines
○ 8 lines
○ 10 lines

 STOP

92

Test 4
Mathematics
Problem Solving

Administration Time: 60 minutes

Distribute scratch paper to the students.

Say Turn to the Test Practice section of your book on page 93. This is Test 4 Mathematics Problem Solving.

Check to see that the students have found page 93.

Say This lesson will check how well you remember the mathematics skills you practiced in other lessons. Be sure your answer spaces are completely filled in. Press your pencil firmly so your marks come out dark. Completely erase any marks for answers that you change. Do not write anything except your answers in your book.

Find Sample A at the top of the page. Look at the answers and listen to the problem. *How many cups of juice are in the pitcher?* Mark the space for your answer.

Allow time for the students to fill in their answers.

Say You should have filled in the space under the second answer for Sample A. If you chose another answer, erase yours completely and fill in the second answer now.

Check to see that the students have marked the correct space.

Say Now do Sample B. Look at the answer choices. Cary drew four shapes. *Which shape is a triangle?* Mark under the shape that is a triangle.

Allow time for the students to fill in their answers.

Say You should have filled in the space under the first shape. If you chose another answer, erase yours completely and fill in the first answer now.

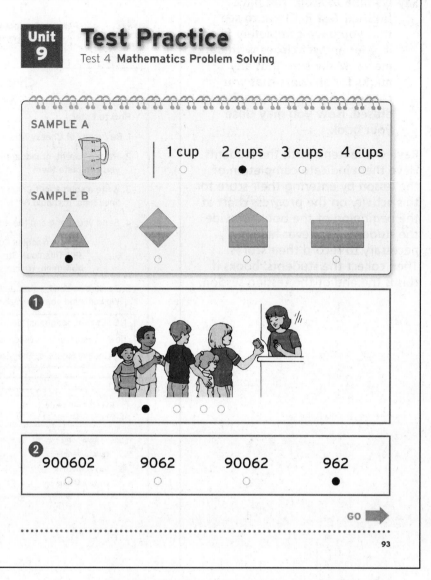

SAMPLE A

1 cup   2 cups   3 cups   4 cups

SAMPLE B

1

2   900602   9062   90062   962

GO

93

Check to see that the students have marked the correct space.

Say Now you will do more mathematics items. Listen carefully to what I say. If you have to, you may use the scratch paper I gave you. If you are not sure which answer is correct, take your best guess. Completely erase any marks for answers that you change. Do you have any questions? Start working now.

Answer any questions the students may have.

Allow time between items for the students to fill in their answers.

Say Move down to the first set of answers. Which child is fourth from the front of the line? Mark under the child who is fourth from the front of the line.

2. **Go to Number 2. Mark under nine hundred sixty-two.**

   Look at the next page, page 94.

Check to be sure the students are on the right page.

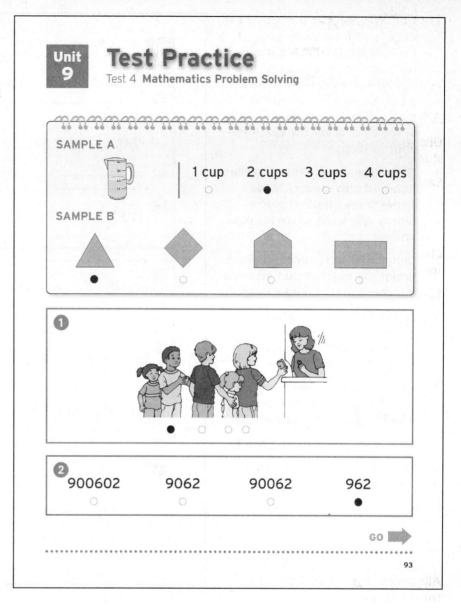

Say Find Number 3 at the top of the page. Listen carefully. Look at the number line. It has marks for numbers, but some of the numbers are missing. There is also a box under one of the marks. Which number should go in the box? Mark the space for your answer.

4. Go to Number 4. What is three hundred plus ninety? Mark under three hundred plus ninety. Mark the space for your answer.

5. Move down to Number 5. Mark under the number that means 6 hundreds, 2 tens, and 8 ones.

6. Look at Number 6. Which answer shows the numbers in order from least to greatest? Mark your answer.

7. What number is one hundred less than five hundred thirty-nine? Mark under your answer.

Look at the next page, page 95.

Check to be sure the students are on the right page.

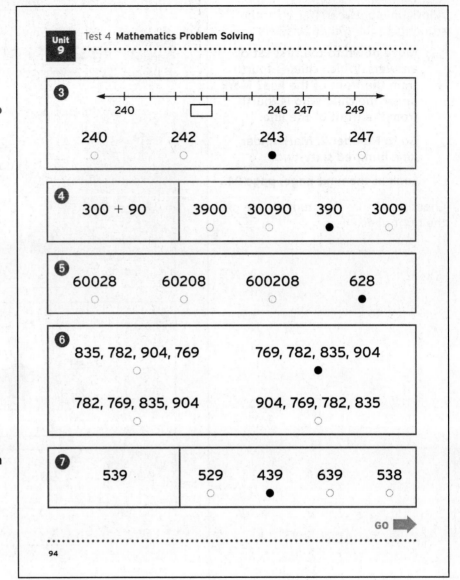

Unit 9 — Test 4 **Mathematics Problem Solving**

3 240   [ ]   246 247   249

240   242   243   247
○   ○   ●   ○

4 300 + 90   3900   30090   390   3009
                     ○   ○   ●   ○

5 60028   60208   600208   628
       ○   ○   ○   ●

6 835, 782, 904, 769   769, 782, 835, 904
              ○   ●

       782, 769, 835, 904   904, 769, 782, 835
              ○   ○

7 539   529   439   639   538
               ○   ●   ○   ○

GO ➡

94

Say Look at Number 8 at the top of the page. Three plus four equals seven is a number sentence that describes this picture of birds. Which sentence also describes the picture? Mark under the answer.

9. Move down to Number 9. What is another way to show five times two? Mark your answer.

10. Look at Number 10. Star wrote this number sentence but forgot one number. What number should go in the box?

11. Move down to Number 11. Mark under the number that goes in the box to make the sentence true.

12. Look at Number 12. Rick was cutting a piece of cake in half. Mark under the piece of cake that has been cut in half.

Look at the next page, page 96.

Check to be sure the students are on the right page. Allow the students a moment to rest.

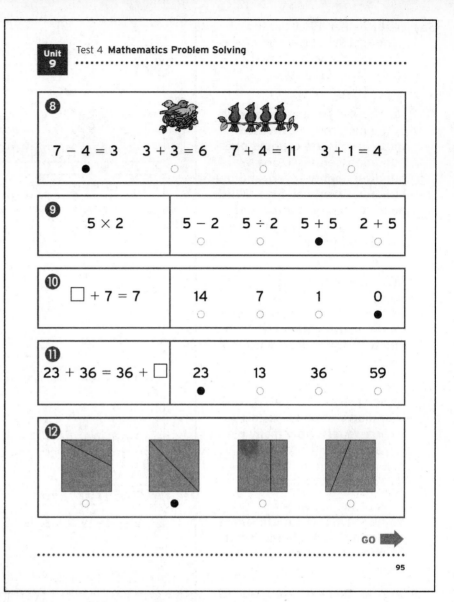

Say Find Number 13 at the top of the page. What fraction of this square is shaded? Mark the space for your answer.

14. Put your finger under Number 14. Look at the pencils in the next row. Eli counted these pencils. He counted one hundred twenty-six, one hundred twenty-seven, and one hundred twenty-eight ... Which pencil would be number one hundred forty? Mark under the pencil that would be one hundred forty.

15. Move down to Number 15. The numbers on the houses follow a pattern. What number belongs on the house without a number? Mark under your answer.

16. Look at Number 16. Greg had fifteen pieces of paper. He used four pieces of paper for his science report. How many pieces of paper did he have left? He had fifteen and he used four. Mark under your answer.

17. Look at the answers for Number 17. This pattern shows skip counting by threes. What number should go in the empty box?

Look at the next page, page 97.

Check to be sure the students are on the right page.

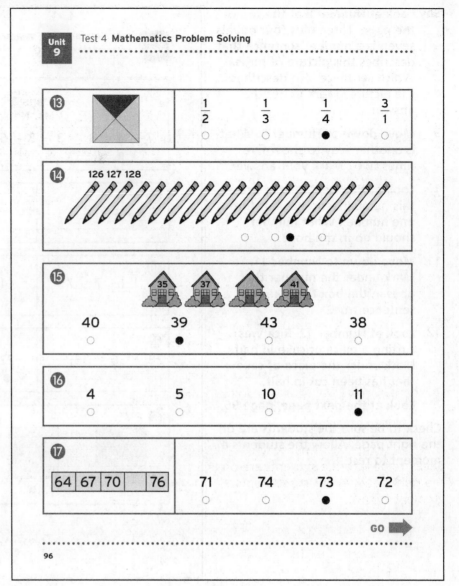

Say Look at the graph at the top of the page. This graph shows how many cans a class collected each day for a canned-food drive. Use the graph to answer Questions 18 and 19.

Put your finger under the first row of answers on the page. Mark under the day on which the class collected exactly twelve cans.

19. Move your finger under the next row. On Tuesday and Wednesday, how many cans did the class collect in all? Mark how many cans the class collected in all on Tuesday and Wednesday.

20. Move your finger under Row 20. Rachel made this table after she asked her friends to tell her their favorite sport. How many more of her friends chose basketball than soccer? Mark your answer.

Look at the next page, page 98.

Check to be sure the students are on the right page. Allow the students a moment to rest.

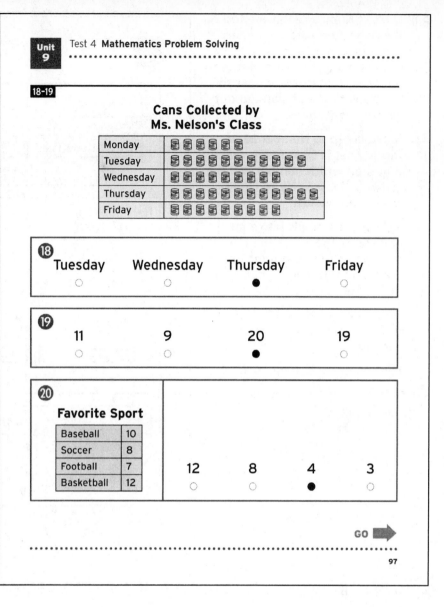

Say Look at Number 21 at the top of the page. The school librarian used these marks to keep track of how many students checked out these books. Mark next to the book that was checked out exactly eight times.

22. Move down to Number 22. If the spinner is spun many, many times, on which number will the arrow be least likely to land? Mark your answer.

23. Kyle put the beads into a jar and shook the jar. Then he took out one bead without looking. Mark under the bead that Kyle most likely picked.

24. Look at Number 24. Mark under the answer that shows two triangles.

Look at the next page, page 99.

Check to be sure the students are on the right page.

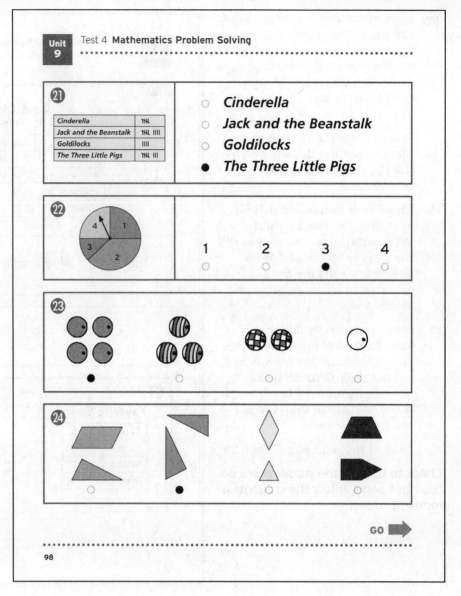

Say Look at Number 25 at the top of the page. Look at the first shape. Which answer has the same number of corners as the first shape? Mark under the shape that has the same number of corners as the first shape.

26. Move down to Number 26. Wendy saw these worms in the garden. Mark under the longest worm.

27. Look at Number 27. Look at the calendar. What day of the week was July sixteenth? Was July sixteenth a Saturday, a Monday, a Tuesday, or a Wednesday?

28. Look at Number 28. Look at the clock. Mark under the time shown on this clock.

Look at the next page, page 100.

Check to be sure the students are on the right page.

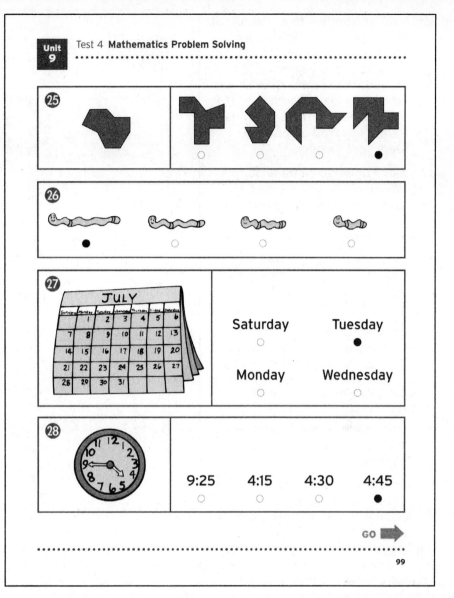

Say Look at Number 29 at the top of the page. Look at the clocks. The first clock shows when Rashid's basketball practice started. The second clock shows when Rashid's basketball practice ended. How long was Rashid's basketball practice? Mark your answer.

30. Move down to Number 30. Which metric unit would be used to measure the height of a school building? Would it be meter, liter, gram, or kilogram?

31. Look at Number 31. How many times longer is the ribbon than the safety pin? Mark your answer.

It's time to stop. You have completed Test 4. Check to see that you have completely filled in your answer circles with dark marks. Make sure that any marks for answers that you changed have been completely erased. Now you may close your book.

Review the items with the students. Have them indicate completion of the lesson by entering their score for this activity on the progress chart at the beginning of the book. Provide the students whatever help is necessary to record their scores. Then collect the students' books if this is the end of the testing session.

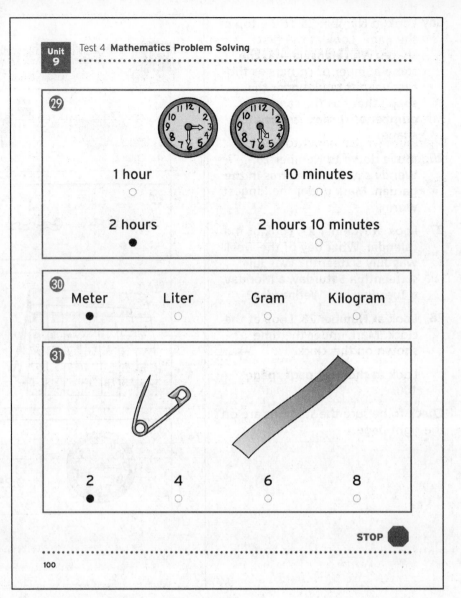

Administration Time: 25 minutes

Distribute scratch paper to the students.

Say Turn to the Test Practice section of your book on page 101. This is Test 5 Mathematics Procedures.

Check to see that the students have found page 101.

Say This lesson will see how well you remember how to solve mathematics computation and word problems. Be sure your answer spaces are completely filled in. Press your pencil firmly so your marks come out dark. Completely erase any marks for answers that you change.

Find Sample A at the top of the page. Katy carried five books in her backpack. Andy carried three books in his backpack. How many books did they carry altogether? Mark the space for your answer.

Allow time for the students to fill in their answers.

Say You should have filled in the space under the third answer, *8.* If you chose another answer, erase yours and fill in the third space now.

Check to see that the students have marked the correct space.

Say Now do Sample B. How much is seven take away three? Is the answer *two, three, ten, eleven,* or is the answer *not here?* Mark your answer.

Allow time for the students to fill in their answers.

Say You should have filled in the space under the last answer, *NH,* because seven take away three is *four,* but *four* is not one of the answer choices. If you chose another answer, erase yours and fill in the last space now.

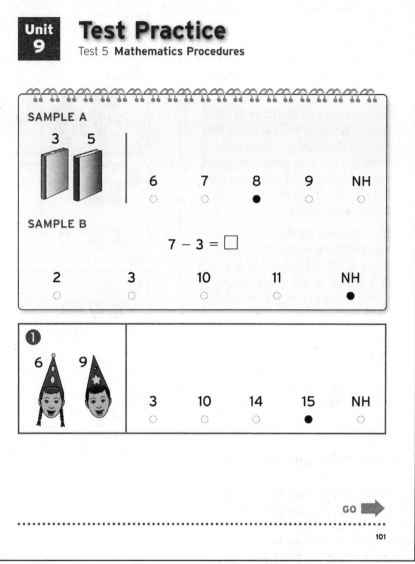

Check to see that the students have marked the correct space.

Say Now you will do more mathematics problems. You may use the scratch paper I gave you. When you fill in your answers, make sure you fill in the spaces completely with dark marks. Completely erase any marks for answers you change. Let's begin.

Allow time between items for the students to fill in their answers.

Say Put your finger under the first problem. Six girls were at Sandy's birthday part. Nine boys were at the party. Mark under how many children were at the party in all.

Look at the next page, page 102.

Check to be sure the students are on the right page. Allow the students a moment to rest.

Say Look at Number 2 at the top of the page. Some students in a nature study class saw 33 birds on Tuesday and 23 birds on Wednesday. How many did they see on both days? Mark under your answer.

3. Move down to Number 3. John had fifty-eight stickers in a box. He put thirteen of them on a letter to his grandmother. How many stickers did John have in his box then? Mark the space under your answer.

4. Move down to Number 4. Fernhill Park had twenty-six trees. Eight of them blew down in a storm. Mark under how many trees are left at Fernhill Park.

5. Look at Number 5. Clancy had sixty-three sheets of colored paper. He used twenty-nine of the sheets of paper in an art project. How many sheets of paper did Clancy have left after his art project?

Look at the next page, page 103.

Check to be sure the students are on the right page. Allow the students a moment to rest.

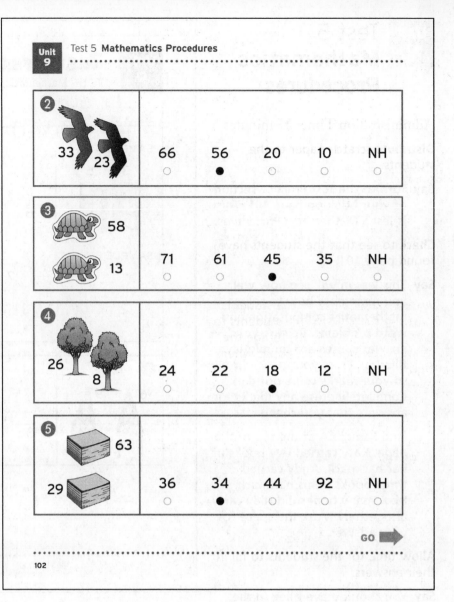

② 33 23

66 ○   56 ●   20 ○   10 ○   NH ○

③ 58 13

71 ○   61 ○   45 ●   35 ○   NH ○

④ 26 8

24 ○   22 ○   18 ●   12 ○   NH ○

⑤ 63 29

36 ○   34 ●   44 ○   92 ○   NH ○

GO ➡

102

Say You will do the rest of the
problems in this part of the Test
Practice by yourself. Look at the
problem and find the answer.
You can work on scratch paper
if you would like. If the answer
you find is not one of the
choices, mark the last space,
NH. When you come to a GO
sign at the bottom of a page,
go on to the next page and
continue working. Work until
you come to the STOP sign at
the bottom of page 104. Do you
have any questions? Start
working now.

Answer any questions the students
have. Allow time for the students to
complete the items. Encourage the
students to use scratch paper when
this is appropriate.

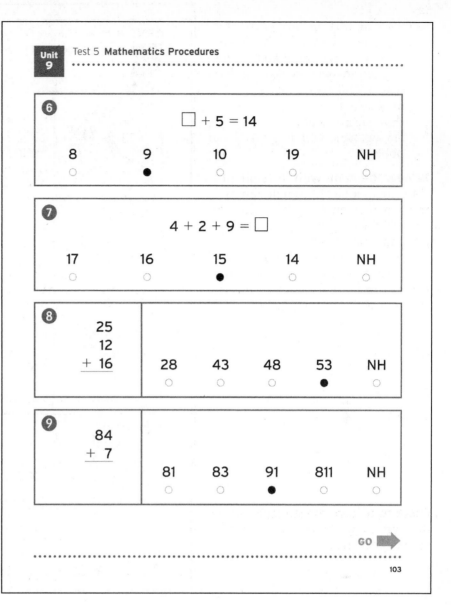

Say It's time to stop. You have completed Test 5. Check to see that you have completely filled in your answer circles with dark marks. Make sure that any marks for answers that you changed have been completely erased. Now you may close your book.

Review the items with the students. Have them indicate completion of the lesson by entering their score for this activity on the progress chart at the beginning of the book. Provide the students whatever help is necessary to record their scores. Then collect the students' books if this is the end of the testing session.

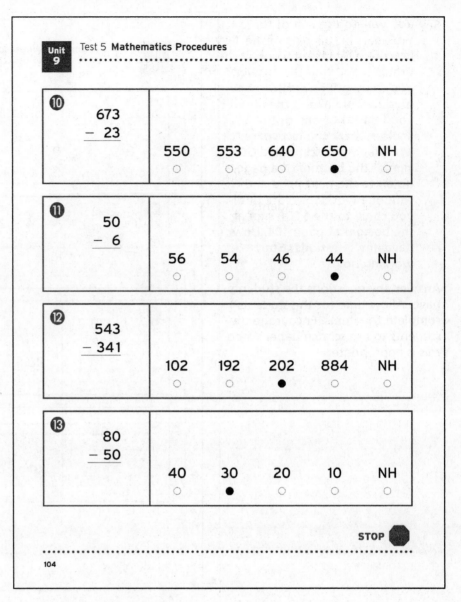

Unit 9 Test 5 **Mathematics Procedures**

⑩
673
− 23

550 ○ 553 ○ 640 ○ 650 ● NH ○

⑪
50
− 6

56 ○ 54 ○ 46 ○ 44 ● NH ○

⑫
543
− 341

102 ○ 192 ○ 202 ● 884 ○ NH ○

⑬
80
− 50

40 ○ 30 ● 20 ○ 10 ○ NH ○

STOP

104

Administration Time: 15 minutes

Say Turn to the Test Practice section of your book on page 105. This is Test 6 Spelling.

Check to see that the students have found page 105.

Say This lesson will check how well you remember the spelling skills you practiced before. Be sure your answer spaces are completely filled in. Press your pencil firmly so your marks come out dark. Completely erase any marks for answers that you change. Do not write anything except your answers in your book.

Let's do Sample A. Read the sentence to yourself as I read it aloud. *My cat ate the whule can of food.* Which word is misspelled? Mark the space for your answer.

Allow time for the students to fill in their answers.

Say The second underlined word is spelled wrong. The correct spelling of the word is *w-h-o-l-e.* If you chose another answer, erase yours and fill in the space under the second answer now.

Check to see that the students have marked the correct space.

Say Now do Sample B. Read the sentence to yourself as I read it aloud. *You can have a bol of soup for lunch.* Which word is misspelled? Mark the space for your answer.

Allow time for the students to fill in their answers.

Say The first underlined word is spelled wrong. The correct spelling of the word is *b-o-w-l.* If you chose another answer, erase yours and fill in the space under the first answer now.

Check to see that the students have marked the correct space.

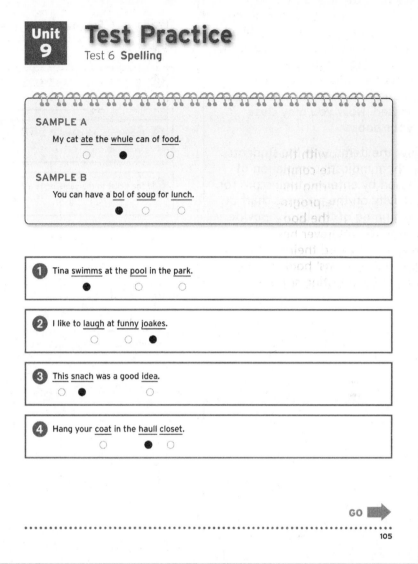

Say Now you will do more spelling items yourself. Look for the underlined word that is spelled wrong. When you mark your answers, make sure you fill in the spaces with dark marks. Do not write anything except your answer choices in your book. Completely erase any marks for answers that you change. When you come to the GO sign at the bottom of the page, go on to the next page and continue working. Work until you come to the STOP sign on page 106. Do you have any questions? Start working now.

Allow time for the students to fill in their answers. Walk around the room and provide test-taking tips as necessary.

Say It's time to stop. You have completed Test 6. Check to see that you have completely filled in your answer circles with dark marks. Make sure that any marks for answers that you changed have been completely erased. Now you may close your book.

Review the items with the students. Have them indicate completion of the lesson by entering their score for this activity on the progress chart at the beginning of the book. Provide the students whatever help is necessary to record their scores. Then collect the students' books if this is the end of the testing session.

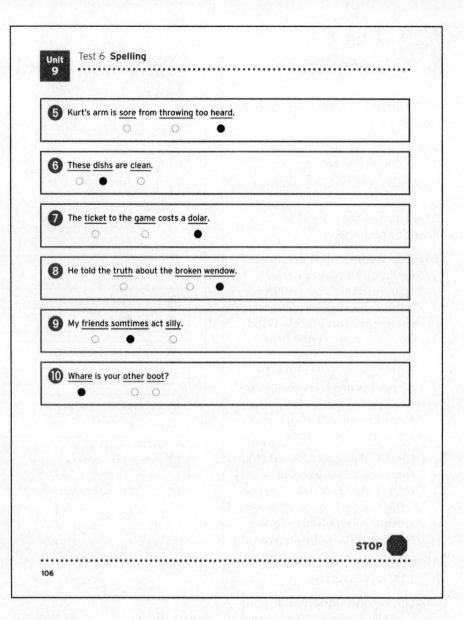

Test 7 Language

Administration Time: 45 minutes

Say Turn to the Test Practice section of your book on page 107. This is Test 7 Language.

Check to see that the students have found page 107.

Say This lesson will check how well you remember the English language skills you practiced in other lessons. Be sure your answer spaces are completely filled in. Press your pencil firmly so your marks come out dark. Completely erase any marks for answers that you change. Do not write anything except your answers in your book.

Find Sample A at the top of the page. Read the sentence with the underlined part to yourself while I read it aloud. "Why are we going to the store." How should the underlined part be written? Look carefully at the capitalization and punctuation of the answers. If the underlined part is correct, choose the last answer, *The way it is.* Mark the space for your answer.

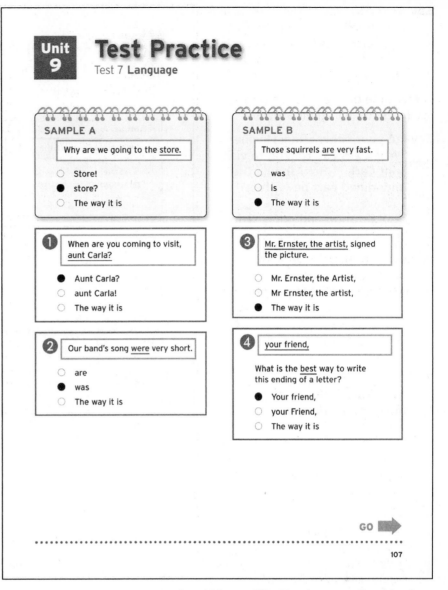

Allow time for the students to fill in their answers.

Say You should have filled in the space beside the second answer. If you chose another answer, erase yours and fill in the second space now.

Check to see that the students have marked the correct space.

Say Now do Sample B. Read the sentence with the underlined part to yourself while I read it aloud. "Those squirrels <u>are</u> very fast." How should the underlined part be written? Should it be *was … is …* or should it be written *The way it is?* Mark the space for your answer.

Allow time for the students to fill in their answers.

Say You should have filled in the space beside the last answer because the underlined part is correct *The way it is.* If you chose another answer, erase yours and fill in the last space now.

Check to see that the students have marked the correct space.

Say Now you will do more items like the samples. Read the items to yourself while I read them aloud. Mark the space for the answer you think is correct.

Allow time between items for the students to fill in their answers.

Say Put your finger under Number 1. "When are you coming to visit, <u>aunt Carla?</u>" How should the underlined part be written? Look very closely at the capitalization and punctuation and then mark your answer.

2. Move down to Number 2. "Our band's song <u>were</u> very short." How should the underlined part be written? Should it be *are* ... *was* ... or should it be written *The way it is?* Mark your answer.

3. Move over to Number 3. "<u>Mr. Ernster, the artist,</u> signed the picture." How should the underlined part be written? Look carefully at the capitalization and punctuation of the answer choices and then mark your answer.

4. Move down to Number 4. "What is the <u>best</u> way to write this ending of a letter? <u>your friend,</u>" Look very closely at the capitalization of the answer choices and then mark your answer.

    Look at the next page, page 108.

Check to be sure the students are on the right page.

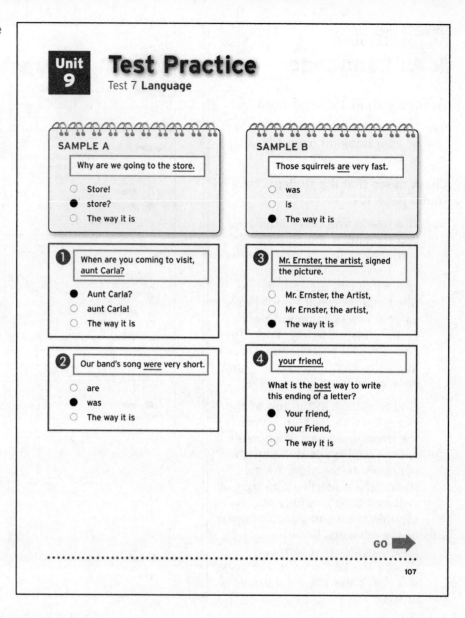

Say Put your finger under Number 5 at the top of the page. "I <u>dont</u> want to see that movie." How should the underlined part be written? Look carefully at the punctuation and mark your answer.

6. Move down to Number 6. "Hey, Cary! Watch out for the <u>ball?</u>" How should the underlined part be written? Look carefully at the capitalization and punctuation of the answer choices. Mark your answer.

7. Move down to Number 7. "Our first snowstorm this year was in <u>october.</u>" How should the underlined part be written? Look carefully at the capitalization and punctuation. Mark your answer.

8. Move down to Number 8. "My apartment is the first one on the second <u>floor.</u>" How should the underlined part be written? Look very closely at the punctuation and then mark your answer.

9. Look at Number 9 in the next column. "The clown <u>gived Sandra</u> a red balloon." Should the underlined part be written *gave Sandra* with a capital S ... *gived sandra* with a small s ... or should it be written *The way it is?* Mark your answer.

10. Move down to Number 10. "My uncle took us camping on <u>Larch mountain.</u>" How should the underlined part be written? Look very closely at the capitalization and punctuation and then mark your answer.

11. Move down to Number 11. "Joshua's cousins live in <u>Chicago Illinois.</u>" How should the underlined part be written? Look very closely at the capitalization and punctuation and then mark your answer.

12. Move down to Number 12. "Have you ever ridden on a <u>horse?</u>" How should the underlined part be written? Look very closely at the capitalization and punctuation and then mark your answer.

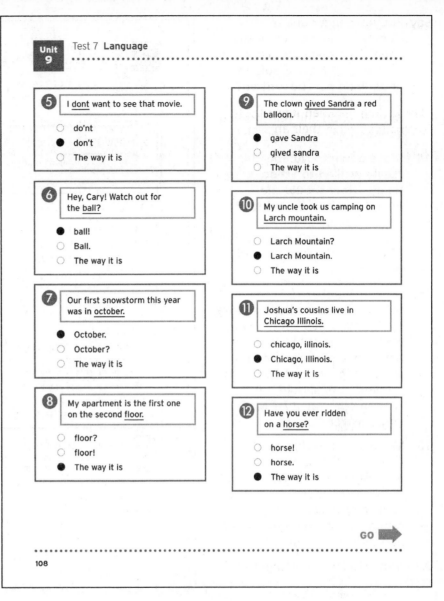

Look at the next page, page 109.

Check to be sure the students are on the right page. Allow the students a moment to rest.

Say Put your finger under Number 13 at the top of the page. "The team's practice will <u>start soon?</u>" How should the underlined part be written? Look carefully at the capitalization and punctuation and mark your answer.

14. Move down to Number 14. "Layla walked to <u>School with Haley.</u>" How should the underlined part be written? Look carefully at the capitalization and punctuation of the answer choices. Mark your answer.

15. Look at Number 15 in the next column. "I was so happy when my grandmother <u>sends</u> me a card." How should the underlined part be written? Should it be written *sent … is sending …* or should it be written *The way it is?* Mark your answer.

16. Move down to Number 16. "'<u>Laura's Wish</u>' is a very interesting story." How should the underlined part be written? Look very closely at the capitalization and punctuation and then mark your answer.

Allow the students a moment to rest.

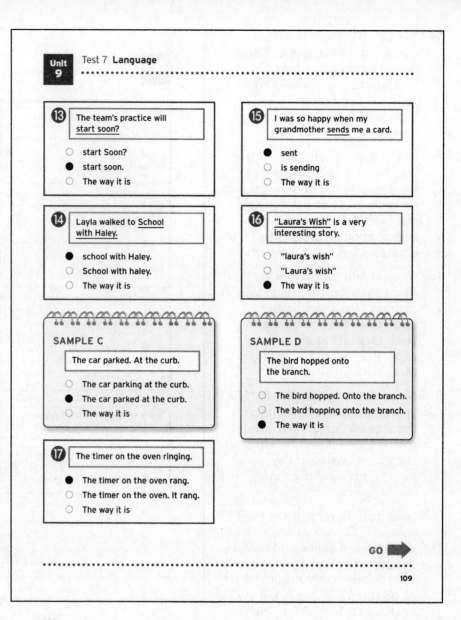

Say Look at Sample C in the box in the middle of the page. Read the group of words in the box while I read it aloud. "The car parked. At the curb." How should this group of words be written to make a complete and correct sentence? Should it be written *The car parking at the curb.* ... *The car parked at the curb.* ... or is it correct *The way it is?* Mark your answer.

Allow time for the students to fill in their answers.

Say The space beside the second answer should be filled in. If you chose another answer, erase yours and fill in the second space now.

Check to see that the students have filled in the correct answer space.

Say Move over to Sample D. Read the group of words in the box while I read it aloud. "The bird hopped onto the branch." How should this group of words be written to make a complete and correct sentence? Should it be written *The bird hopped. Onto the branch.* ... *The bird hopping onto the branch.* ... or is the group of words correct *The way it is?* Mark your answer.

Allow time for the students to fill in their answers.

Say The space for the third answer should be filled in because the group of words is correct *The way it is.* If you chose another answer, erase yours and fill in the second space now.

Check to see that the students have filled in the correct answer space.

Say Now we will do more items like Samples C and D. Read each sentence in the box to yourself while I read it aloud. Find the answer choice that is the best way to write the sentence or choose *The way it is.* Let's begin.

Allow time between items for the students to fill in their answers.

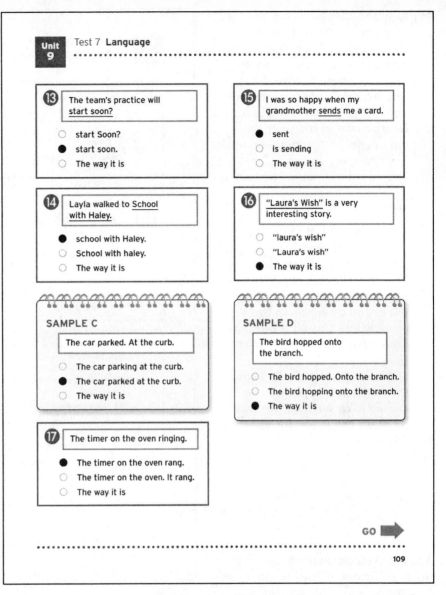

Say Find Number 17 below the Samples. Read the group of words in the box while I read it aloud. "The timer on the oven ringing." How should the group of words in the box be written? Should it be written *The timer on the oven rang.* ... *The timer on the oven. It rang.* ... or should it be written *The way it is?* Mark the space for your answer.

Turn to the next page, page 110.

Check to be sure the students have found the right page.

Say Move to Number 18 at the top of the page. Read the group of words in the box while I read it aloud. "Ducks swim in the river near my house." How should the group of words in the box be written? Should it be written *Ducks swim in the river. Near my house. ... Ducks swim. In the river near my house. ...* or should it be written *The way it is?* Mark the space for your answer.

19. Move down to Number 19. Read the group of words in the box while I read it aloud. "Students drawing pictures about their visit to the park." How should the group of words in the box be written? Should it be written *Students drew pictures about their visit. To the park. ... Students drew pictures about their visit to the park. ...* or should it be written *The way it is?* Mark the space for your answer.

20. Look at Number 20. Read the group of words in the box while I read it aloud. "My mother is a teacher at the school down the street." How should the group of words in the box be written? Should it be written *My mother is a teacher. At the school down the street. ... My mother being a teacher at the school down the street. ...* or should it be written *The way it is?* Mark the space for your answer.

21. Look at Number 21 in the next column. Read the group of words in the box while I read it aloud. "At the zoo. Will learned about elephants." How should the group of words in the box be written? Should it be written *At the zoo, Will learned about elephants. ... At the zoo, Will learning about elephants. ...* or should it be written *The way it is?* Mark the space for your answer.

22. Look at Number 22. Read the group of words in the box while I read it aloud. "Because it was Tuesday. I went to music class after school." How should the group of words in the box be written? Should it be written *Because it was Tuesday, I going to music class after school. ... Because it was Tuesday, I went*

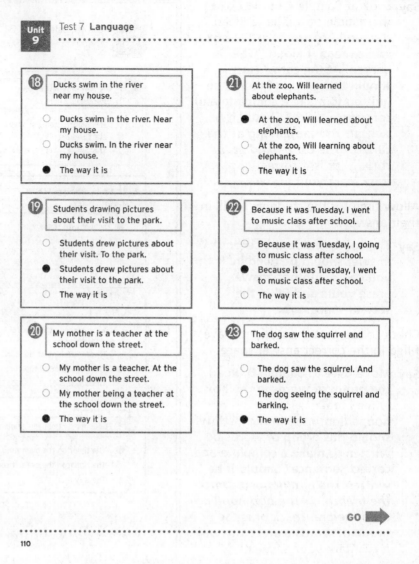

to music class after school. ... or should it be written *The way it is?* Mark the space for your answer.

23. Look at Number 23. Read the group of words in the box while I read it aloud. "The dog saw the squirrel and barked." How should the group of words in the box be written? Should it be written *The dog saw the squirrel. And barked. ... The dog seeing the squirrel and barking. ...* or should it be written *The way it is?* Mark the space for your answer.

Look at the next page, page 111.

Check to be sure the students are on the right page. Allow the students a moment to rest.

Say Find Number 24 at the top of the page. Read the group of words in the box while I read it aloud. "My clothes were soaked. By the hard rain." How should the group of words in the box be written? Should it be written *My clothes being soaked by the hard rain. ... My clothes were soaked by the hard rain. ...* or should it be written *The way it is*? Mark the space for your answer.

25. Move down to Number 25. Read the group of words in the box while I read it aloud. "Sam's parents sing in a band. With their friends." How should the group of words in the box be written? Should it be written *Sam's parents they sing in a band with their friends. ... Sam's parents sing in a band with their friends. ...* or should it be written *The way it is*? Mark the space for your answer.

26. Look at Number 26 in the next column. Read the group of words in the box while I read it aloud. "Kyle asked a question and waited for the answer." How should the group of words in the box be written? Should it be written *Kyle asked a question. Waiting for the answer. ... Kyle asking a question. He waited for the answer. ...* or should it be written *The way it is*? Mark the space for your answer.

    Look at the next page, page 112.

Check to be sure the students are on the right page. Allow the students a moment to rest.

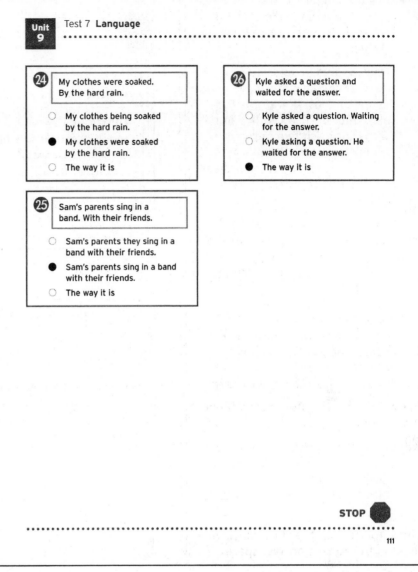

Say Let's do Samples E and F at the top of the page. Follow along as I read the paragraph for the samples.

"Fish can live in saltwater or freshwater. Saltwater fish live in oceans or seas. If water is too salty, then no fish can live in it. Freshwater fish live in rivers and lakes. Some fish, like salmon, spend part of their lives in saltwater and part in freshwater."

Now look at the question for Sample E. Read the question to yourself while I read it aloud. "Which of these would go <u>best</u> after the last sentence?" *No matter where fish live, the water has to be clean. … Fish come in thousands of different shapes and sizes. … Did you know that some lakes are salty?* Mark the space for your answer.

Allow time for the students to fill in their answers.

Say The space for the first answer should be filled in. If you chose another answer, erase yours and fill in the first answer space now.

Check to see that the students have filled in the correct answer space.

Say Now look at the question for Sample F. Read the question to yourself while I read it aloud. "Why was this story written?" The answers are *To tell about oceans … To tell where fish live … To tell about salmon.* Mark the space for your answer.

Allow time for the students to fill in their answers.

Say The space for the second answer should be filled in. If you chose another answer, erase yours and fill in the second answer space now.

Check to see that the students have filled in the correct answer space.

Say Now you will do more items. Listen carefully to what I say while you read the paragraphs and the items to yourself. Choose the answer you think is best. Let's begin.

Allow time between items for the students to fill in their answers.

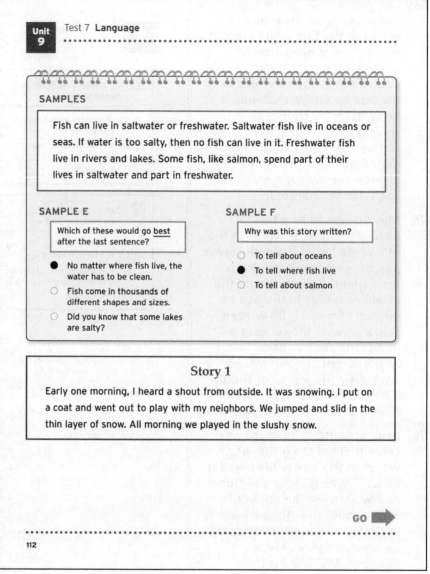

Unit 9 Test 7 **Language**

SAMPLES

Fish can live in saltwater or freshwater. Saltwater fish live in oceans or seas. If water is too salty, then no fish can live in it. Freshwater fish live in rivers and lakes. Some fish, like salmon, spend part of their lives in saltwater and part in freshwater.

SAMPLE E

Which of these would go <u>best</u> after the last sentence?

● No matter where fish live, the water has to be clean.
○ Fish come in thousands of different shapes and sizes.
○ Did you know that some lakes are salty?

SAMPLE F

Why was this story written?

○ To tell about oceans
● To tell where fish live
○ To tell about salmon

Story 1

Early one morning, I heard a shout from outside. It was snowing. I put on a coat and went out to play with my neighbors. We jumped and slid in the thin layer of snow. All morning we played in the slushy snow.

GO →

112

Say Read along as I read Story 1. The questions will be on the next page.

"Early one morning, I heard a shout from outside. It was snowing. I put on a coat and went out to play with my neighbors. We jumped and slid in the thin layer of snow. All morning we played in the slushy snow. "

Look at the next page, page 113.

Check to be sure the students are on the right page. Allow the students a moment to rest.

27. **Look at Number 27.** "Which of these would go <u>best</u> after the last sentence?" *I like playing with my neighbors. ... Each snowflake has a different pattern. ... We had fun until the snow melted.* Mark your answer.

28. **Look at Number 28.** "Which of these would <u>not</u> go with this story?" *There wasn't enough snow to make a snowman. ... My neighbor, Colin, likes to go skiing when it snows. ... It doesn't snow around here very often.* Mark your answer.

    Read along as I read Story 2. There will be two questions about the story.

    "When Kevin gets to the beach, he rushes over the sand to the high tide mark. That's where the waves leave a big pile of seaweed. Kevin likes to poke through the pile. He finds shells and pieces of driftwood."

29. **Look at Number 29.** "Which of these would go <u>best</u> after the last sentence?" *One time Kevin found a glass float from a fishing net. ... Each high tide leaves its own mark on the beach. ... Kevin's sisters like to build sandcastles.* Mark your answer.

30. **Look at Number 30.** "Which of these would <u>not</u> go with this story?" *Sometimes the seaweed smells bad, but he doesn't care. ... Seaweed is food for some of the animals in the ocean. ... The driftwood he finds is smooth and silvery.* Mark your answer.

    Look at the next page, page 114.

Check to be sure the students are on the right page.

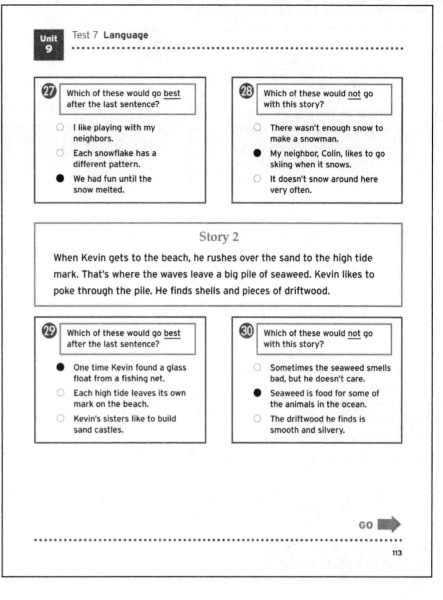

Say Look at Story 3 at the top of the page. Read along as I read the story.

"The car was packed. Mom said, 'Load up!' and everyone climbed in. Ben watched out the window as they passed trees and fields. All day the family drove. At night, they set up their tent. Ben stared at the stars. 'I like this trip,' he said."

31. Look at Number 31. "Why was this story written?" *To tell how far a family drove ... To tell about a trip ... To tell why Ben likes camping.* Mark your answer.

32. Look at Number 32. "Which of these would go <u>best</u> after the last sentence?" *Ben hoped they could go camping again. ... Ben got tired of sitting still in the car. ... Mom and Dad sang songs while they drove.* Mark the space for your answer.

33. Look at Number 33. "Which of these would <u>not</u> go with this story?" *The tent fell over twice before they got it right. ... Ben's dad had just taught him how to swim. ... The car was full of sleeping bags and folding chairs.* Mark your answer.

Look at the next page, page 115.

Check to be sure the students are on the right page. Allow the students a moment to rest.

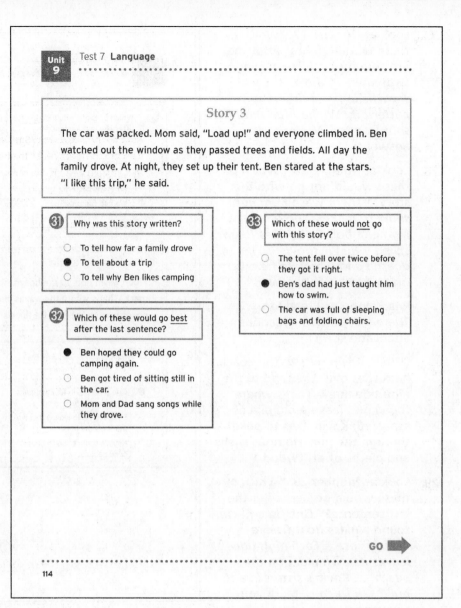

Say Look at Story 4 at the top of the page. Read along as I read the story.

"Aunt Sophie likes music. She wants to play the guitar, so she is taking lessons. She practices all the time, and she can already play songs. She taught me the words so I can sing along."

34. Put your finger under the question for Number 34. "Which of these would go <u>best</u> after the last sentence?" *Her teacher says that practice is very important. … Aunt Sophie likes to dance to music on the radio. … Aunt Sophie and I have fun making music together.* Mark the space for your answer.

35. Move down to Number 35. "Why was this story written?" *To tell how to play a guitar … To tell what Aunt Sophie learned to do … To tell what songs Aunt Sophie likes.* Mark your answer.

36. Look at Number 36. "Which of these would <u>not</u> go with this story?" *I like singing while Aunt Sophie plays. … Some of the songs have words. … Aunt Sophie lives a few blocks away.* Mark your answer.

Turn to the next page, page 116.

Check to be sure the students are on the right page.

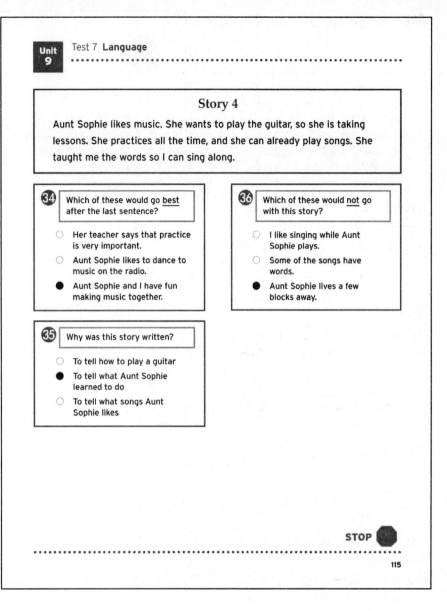

Say Now we will do a different kind of item. Find Sample G at the top of the page. Read the question to yourself while I read it aloud. "Reena is making a shopping list for the grocery store. Which of these does not belong on her list?" The answers are *Milk … Bread …* or *Radio?* Mark the space for your answer.

Allow time for the students to fill in their answers.

Say The space for the last answer should be filled in. If you chose another answer, erase yours and fill in the last answer space now.

Check to see that the students have filled in the correct answer space.

Say Move over to Sample H. Read the question to yourself while I read it aloud. "Bart is writing a story about making cookies. Which idea should be first?" Should it be *Eating the tasty cookies … Mixing everything together … Putting the cookies in the oven?* Mark the space for your answer.

Allow time for the students to fill in their answers.

Say The space for the second answer should be filled in. If you chose another answer, erase yours and fill in the second answer space now.

Check to see that the students have marked the correct space.

Say Now you will do more items like Samples G and H. I will read the the question and the answer choices aloud while you read to yourself. When I have finished reading, you will mark the space for your answer. Let's begin.

Allow time between items for students to fill in their answers.

Say Find Number 37 below the samples. "Peggy is writing a letter to a friend describing her town park. Which of these belongs in her letter?" Is it *The kinds of trees in the park … The street names in her town … The weather this time of year?* Mark the space for your answer.

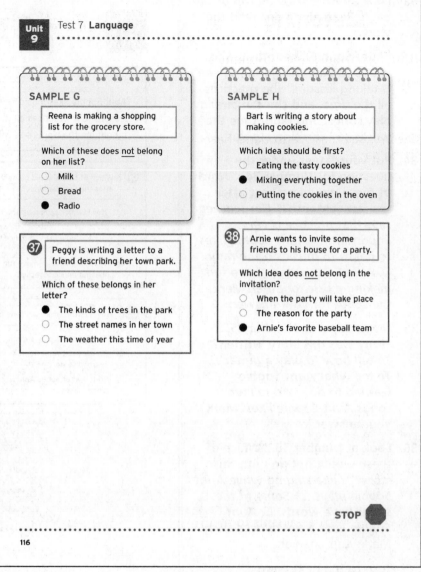

38. Move over to Number 38. "Arnie wants to invite some friends to his house for a party. Which idea does not belong in the invitation?" The answers are *When the party will take place … The reason for the party … Arnie's favorite baseball team.* Mark your answer.

Say It's time to stop. You have completed Test 7. Check to see that you have completely filled in your answer circles with dark marks. Make sure that any marks for answers that you changed have been completely erased. Now you may close your book.

Review the items with the students. Have them indicate completion of the lesson by entering their score for this activity on the progress chart at the beginning of the book. Provide the students whatever help is necessary to record their scores. Then collect the students' books if this is the end of the testing session.

Administration Time: 35 minutes

Say Turn to the Test Practice section of your book on page 117. This is Test 8 Listening.

Check to see that the students have found page 117.

Say This lesson will check how well you remember the listening skills you practiced in other lessons. Be sure your answer spaces are completely filled in. Press your pencil firmly so your marks come out dark. Completely erase any marks for answers that you change. Do not write anything except your answers in your book.

Listen carefully to what I say as you look at the answer choices for Sample A in the box. Pay attention now.

I helped *bathe* my baby brother. *Bathe* means the same as— *dress … feed … wash.* Which word means the same as *bathe?* Mark the space for your answer.

Allow time for the students to fill in their answers.

Say The correct answer is *wash. Bathe* and *wash* mean about the same thing. If you chose another answer, erase yours completely and fill in the space beside *wash* now.

Check to see that the students have marked the correct space.

Say Move down to Sample B. Look at the answer choices. Listen carefully to what I say.

Some butterflies use bright colors to *fool* birds. To *fool* means to—*warn … call … trick.* Mark the space for your answer.

Allow time for the students to fill in their answers.

Say The last answer, *trick,* is correct. If you chose another answer, erase yours completely and fill in the last answer space now.

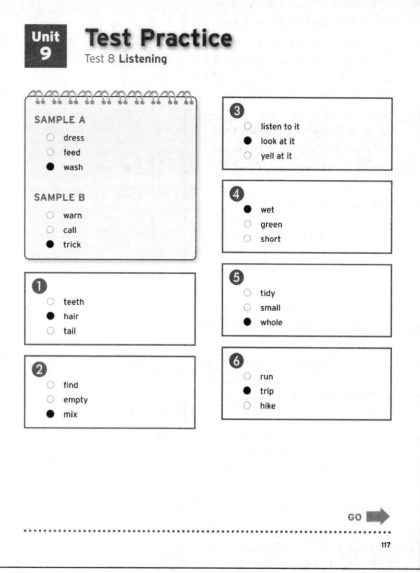

Check to see that the students have marked the correct space.

Say Now you will do more items. They are just like the sample items we did. Listen carefully to what I say as you look at the answer choices. Fill in your answer spaces with dark marks and completely erase any marks for answers that you change. Do you have any questions? Let's begin.

Pause between items to allow time for students to fill in their answers.

1. Now look at the first group of answers. Seals have very thick *fur.* An animal's *fur* is its—*teeth ... hair ... tail.*

2. Move down to the next group, Group 2. Eileen *combined* two bags of marbles. To combine is to—*find ... empty ... mix.* Mark your answer

3. Maria *glanced* at the delivery truck. To *glance* at something means to—*listen to it ... look at it ... yell at it.*

4. Look at the answers for Number 4. The grass was very *damp.* Damp means the same as—*wet ... green ... short.* Mark your answer.

5. Casey weeded the *entire* vegetable garden. *Entire* means the same as—*tidy ... small ... whole.*

6. Move down to Number 6. I *stumbled* on the rocky trail. To *stumble* means to—*run ... trip ... hike.*

    Turn to the next page, page 118.

Check to see that the students have found the right page. Allow a moment for students to relax.

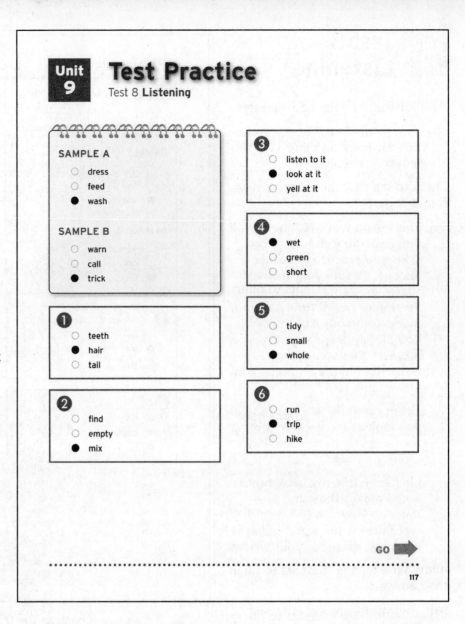

Say Find the box with Sample C at the top of the page. Look at the pictures of Robert and his sister. Listen to this story to see how Robert and his sister get to the park.

"Robert," said his little sister, "will you walk to the park with me? We can play in the sandbox with my new dump truck."

Which picture shows how Robert and his sister got to the park? Mark the space for your answer.

Allow time for the students to fill in their answers.

Say You should have filled in the space under the last picture. If you chose another answer, erase yours and fill in the last answer space now.

Check to see that the students have marked the correct space.

Say Now look at Sample D. Listen carefully to what I say. Then mark under the picture you think is right.

What did Robert and his sister probably play with at the park? Was it a—*dump truck* … *shovel and pail* … or *ball*? Mark your answer.

Unit 9
Test 8 **Listening**
SAMPLE C
SAMPLE D
7
8
9
10
11
GO
118

Allow time for the students to fill in their answers.

Say You should have marked the space under the *dump truck* because Robert's sister said they could play with her new dump truck. If you chose another answer, erase yours and fill in the first answer space now.

Check to see that the students have marked the correct space.

Say Now you will do more items.
Listen to the story that I read
and the questions about it.
Mark the space for the answer
you think is correct.

Coloring with crayons is great
fun. Crayons are easy to use,
they're not messy, and the
colors are bright. Crayons are
made from melted wax. Colored
powder is added to the hot wax
to make each color. Then the
wax is poured into tubes
shaped like crayons. When the
wax is cool, each crayon is
given a paper wrapper. Then
they're ready to use. Making
crayons sounds simple, but
good crayons were only
invented 100 years ago. Before
that, children's crayons were
just chalk or clay. They looked
nice, but they didn't work very
well. Two cousins, Edwin Binney
and C. Harold Smith, thought
children would enjoy colored
crayons. They had already
invented a new kind of
blackboard chalk. Now, they
came up with a way to make
wax crayons. Their first box of
crayons had only eight colors
and cost a nickel. The new
crayons were very popular, even
with adult artists.

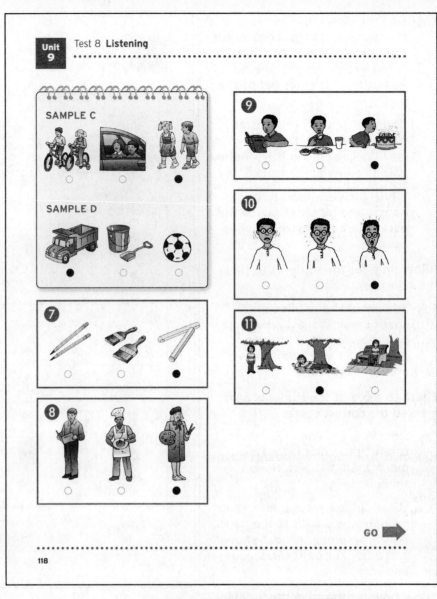

Pause between items to allow time
for students to fill in their answers.

7. Look at Row 7 under the samples. What did
Edwin Binney and C. Harold Smith invent
besides crayons? Was it—*pencils …
paintbrushes …* or *chalk*? Mark your answer.

8. Move down to the next row. Who liked to use
crayons when they were first invented? Was
it—*teachers … cooks …* or *artists*?

Here is another story. There will be three
questions about it.

Matthew walked outside after eating birthday
cake and opening his presents. He almost
tripped on Renatta. "What are you doing lying
in the grass?" He asked her. "Just watching,"
she said, and she pointed to the grass.
Matthew bent down and saw a line of tiny
ants marching through the grass.

9. What had Matthew been doing before he

went outside? Was he—*reading a book …
eating dinner …* or *having a party*?

10. Look at Number 10. How did Matthew
probably look when he saw Renatta lying
down? Was he—*scared … happy …* or
surprised?

11. Move down to the last row. Which picture
shows Renatta when Matthew saw her? Mark
your answer.

Turn to the next page, page 119.

Check to see that the students have found the right
page.

Say Find Sample E in the box at the top of the page. Listen to this story, the question, and the answer choices that follow.

Irene brushed her rabbit outside. Then she took her rabbit inside and sat down by the window. After a few minutes, she saw a small bird land. It picked up some fluffy hair with its beak. Then it flew up into the tree to finish building its home.

Now listen to the question and the answer choices for Sample E. What kind of pet did Irene brush? Was it a—*Dog … Cat … or Rabbit?* Mark your answer.

Allow time for the students to fill in their answers.

Say You should have filled in the space beside the last answer, *rabbit.* If you chose another answer, erase yours and fill in the last answer space now.

Check to see that the students have marked the correct space.

Say Now move down to Sample F. Listen carefully. Where did the bird take the hair? *To a bush … To a lake … To a nest … To a roof.* Mark the space for your answer.

Allow time for the students to fill in their answers.

Say You should have filled in the space beside the third answer, *to a nest.* If you chose another answer, erase yours and fill in the third answer space now.

Check to see that the students have marked the correct space.

Say Now you will do more items. Listen to each story that I read and the questions about it. Mark the space for your answer.

Making music can be as simple as putting together a few things from around your house. For your noisemaker, you will need a metal can, like a soup can, some small rocks, a plastic bag, and a rubber band. First, get an adult to help you open the can and clean it out. Then, put a handful of small rocks in the

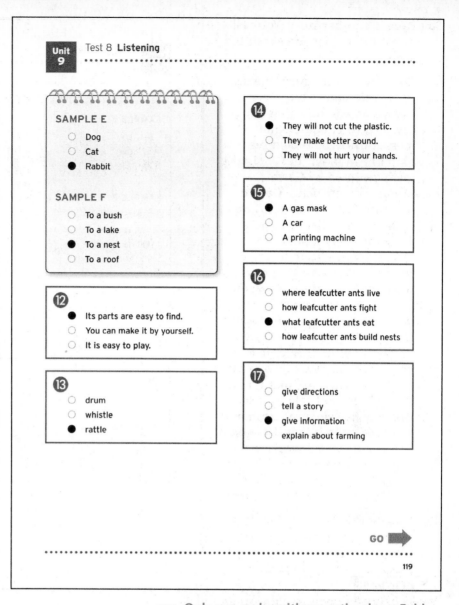

can. Only use rocks with smooth edges. Fold the plastic bag into several layers. It should be big enough to cover the top of the can. Use the rubber band to hold the bag tightly over the top of the can. Shake your noisemaker up, down, or sideways to make different rhythms. With a noisemaker, making music is easy.

12. Look at Number 12, right below the samples. What is one reason a noisemaker is so easy to make? *Its parts are easy to find. … You can make it by yourself. … It is easy to play.*

13. You can tell from the paragraph that a noisemaker is a kind of—*drum … whistle … rattle.*

14. Why should you use rocks with smooth edges in your noisemaker? *They will not cut the plastic. … They make better sound. … They will not hurt your hands.*

Say Here is another story. You will answer one question about the story.

Red means stop; green means go. Traffic signals are everywhere in our cities and towns. Just imagine what a mess traffic would be if we didn't have them. Traffic signals were invented by Garrett Morgan in the 1920s. Garrett Morgan was born in 1877. He didn't have a chance to go to school for very long, but he was always interested in learning. He worked as a sewing machine repairman and started several businesses. He even started a newspaper. More than anything, Garrett Morgan loved to work on machines and try to invent new ones. He made new sewing machines and a gas mask that fire fighters and soldiers used. One day he saw a car crash into a horse-drawn buggy. He went home and started working on a way of controlling traffic. A few years later, his traffic signals were used all over the country.

15. Look at Number 15. What is something this passage says Garret Morgan invented? *A gas mask … A car … A printing machine.*

Here is another story. It is about an interesting insect.

Leafcutter ants aren't like the ants in your backyard. Leafcutter ants climb trees and bite off big pieces of leaves. Each piece weighs much more than an ant, but the ants are amazingly strong. The ants carry the leaves to the nest. Inside a leafcutter nest, special ants cut the leaves into small chunks and line them up in rows. Mushrooms grow on the leaves, and the leafcutter ants eat the mushrooms. Leafcutter ants are farmers!

16. This paragraph mainly tells—*where leafcutter ants live … how leafcutter ants fight … what leafcutter ants eat … how leafcutter ants build nests.*

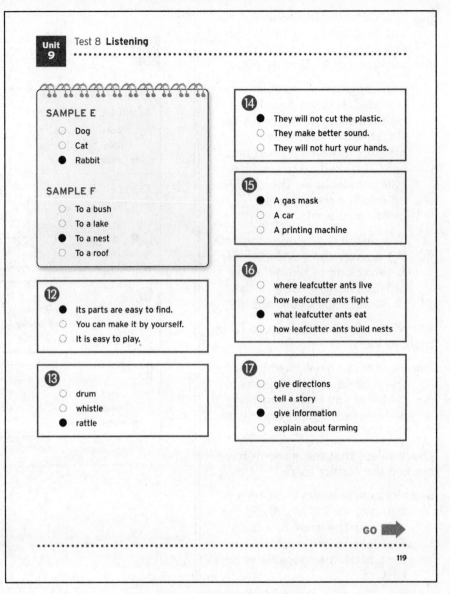

SAMPLE E
○ Dog
○ Cat
● Rabbit

SAMPLE F
○ To a bush
○ To a lake
● To a nest
○ To a roof

12
● Its parts are easy to find.
○ You can make it by yourself.
○ It is easy to play.

13
○ drum
○ whistle
● rattle

14
● They will not cut the plastic.
○ They make better sound.
○ They will not hurt your hands.

15
● A gas mask
○ A car
○ A printing machine

16
○ where leafcutter ants live
○ how leafcutter ants fight
● what leafcutter ants eat
○ how leafcutter ants build nests

17
○ give directions
○ tell a story
● give information
○ explain about farming

GO ➡

119

17. Move down to the last row. The purpose of this paragraph is to—*give directions … tell a story … give information … explain about farming.*

Turn to the next page, page 120.

Check to see that the students have found the right page. Allow the students a moment to relax.

Say Look at the answers in the first column. Listen to Kareem give instructions to Louis.

It's not very hard—just three things to mix together. First, you scoop some yogurt into a bowl. I like vanilla best, but you could use any flavor. Stir the yogurt to make it smooth. Then pick out some fruit. Strawberries and bananas are good to use. They're easy to cut because they're soft. Cut up the fruit and add it to the yogurt. Get some granola or crunchy cereal. Mix some of it with the fruit and yogurt. That's the last thing to remember, because that's all there is to the recipe. I'll go over it again. First, get some yogurt. Next, add some cut-up fruit. Last, stir in some granola.

18. Look at Number 18. What is a good name for this story? Is it— *"Kareem Makes a Cake"* … *"Kareem's Recipe"* … *"Louis Learns to Cook"* … or *"Louis's Idea"*?

19. Are these instructions for making—*yogurt* … *a sandwich* … *a snack* … or *granola*?

20. Move down to Number 20. What does Kareem tell Louis to put the yogurt in? *A cup* … *A pan* … *A jar* … *A bowl.*

21. Move down to Number 21. Does Kareem think these instructions are—*simple* … *difficult* … *scary* … or *funny*?

Look at the answers in the next column.

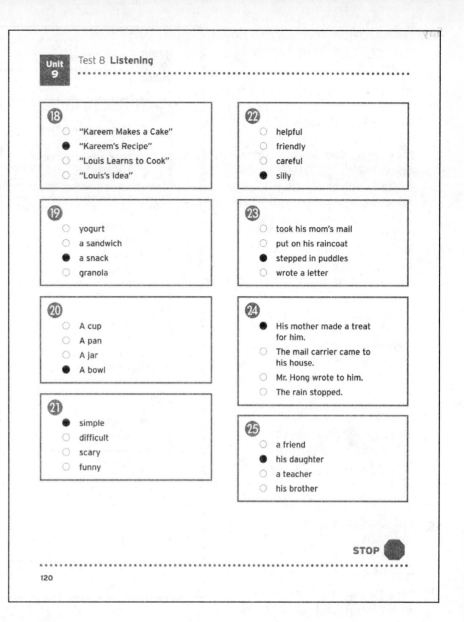

Unit 9   Test 8 **Listening**

18.
○ "Kareem Makes a Cake"
● "Kareem's Recipe"
○ "Louis Learns to Cook"
○ "Louis's Idea"

19.
○ yogurt
○ a sandwich
● a snack
○ granola

20.
○ A cup
○ A pan
○ A jar
● A bowl

21.
● simple
○ difficult
○ scary
○ funny

22.
○ helpful
○ friendly
○ careful
● silly

23.
○ took his mom's mail
○ put on his raincoat
● stepped in puddles
○ wrote a letter

24.
● His mother made a treat for him.
○ The mail carrier came to his house.
○ Mr. Hong wrote to him.
○ The rain stopped.

25.
○ a friend
● his daughter
○ a teacher
○ his brother

STOP

120

Say Listen to this story about a boy who did something for his mother.

Henry saw his mother look out at the rain and frown. "I'll go to the post office for you, Mom," he said. "I like walking in the rain." His mom smiled and handed him the letters to be mailed. Henry put on his raincoat and yellow boots. He went next door to see Mr. Hong. Mr. Hong had a letter to send to his daughter. Henry tucked all the mail under his raincoat so it wouldn't get wet and squished through the puddles to the post office. When Henry got home, his mom handed him a mug of hot chocolate. "Even people who like to walk in the rain deserve a treat," she said.

22. Look at Number 22. All of these words might be used to describe Henry except— *helpful ... friendly ... careful ... silly.*

23. What did Henry do right after visiting Mr. Hong? He—*took his mom's mail ... put on his raincoat ... stepped in puddles ... wrote a letter.*

24. Move down to Number 24. What happened while Henry was at the post office? *His mother made a treat for him. ... The mail carrier came to his house. ... Mr. Hong wrote to him. ... The rain stopped.*

25. Move down to Number 25. Mr. Hong wrote a letter to—*a friend ... his daughter ... a teacher ... his brother.*

It's time to stop. You have completed Test 8. Check to see that you have completely filled in your answer circles with dark marks. Make sure that any marks for answers that you changed have been completely erased. Now you may close your book.

Review the items with the students. Have them indicate completion of the lesson by entering their score for this activity on the progress chart at the beginning of the book. Provide the students whatever help is necessary to record their scores.

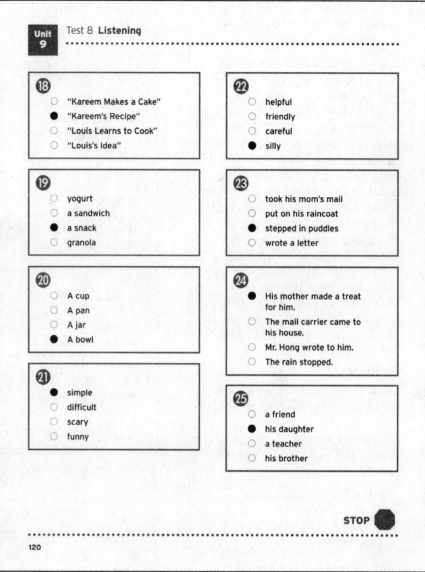

Unit 9 Test 8 Listening

⑱
- ○ "Kareem Makes a Cake"
- ● "Kareem's Recipe"
- ○ "Louis Learns to Cook"
- ○ "Louis's Idea"

⑲
- ○ yogurt
- ○ a sandwich
- ● a snack
- ○ granola

⑳
- ○ A cup
- ○ A pan
- ○ A jar
- ● A bowl

㉑
- ● simple
- ○ difficult
- ○ scary
- ○ funny

㉒
- ○ helpful
- ○ friendly
- ○ careful
- ● silly

㉓
- ○ took his mom's mail
- ○ put on his raincoat
- ● stepped in puddles
- ○ wrote a letter

㉔
- ● His mother made a treat for him.
- ○ The mail carrier came to his house.
- ○ Mr. Hong wrote to him.
- ○ The rain stopped.

㉕
- ○ a friend
- ● his daughter
- ○ a teacher
- ○ his brother

STOP

120

Discuss the tests with the students. Ask if they felt comfortable during the tests or if they were nervous. Which items were most difficult? Which were easiest? Did they understand all the directions? After the tests have been scored, go over any questions that caused difficulty. If necessary, review the skills that will help the students score their highest.